This Other Eden

Christine Hoy

Tale

First Published 2022
Copyright © 2022 Christine Hoy

All rights reserved.
ISBN-13: 978-0-6480386-8-9
ISBN-10: 0-6480386-8-9

National Library of Australia Cataloguing-in-Publication entry
Creator: Hoy, Christine, author.
Title: This Other Eden / Christine Hoy.

Book cover design by RL Sather

Tale Publishing
Melbourne, Australia

INTRODUCTION

Over the past years I have delved into my family history, to discover how it has shaped my own life and what it is that makes me the person I am today. I am the sum total of all those who have come before me.

With licence and imagination, I have recaptured their story, from the early days as agricultural labourers in Oxford, through the industrial revolution, to become men of property in London and affluent farmers in the colonies. This narrative must remain a novel, since I can only assume thoughts, feelings, and emotions that would have been present in the lives of those courageous people who fought poverty, death, disease, and war, with each generation overcoming their own misery, to triumph under the most difficult of circumstances.

Christine Hoy (née Willott)
March 2021

"This Other Eden"

This royal throne of kings, this sceptred isle,
This earth of majesty, this seat of Mars,
This other Eden, demi-paradise,
This fortress built by Nature for herself
Against infection and the hand of war,
This happy breed of men, this little world,
This precious stone set in the silver sea…
This blessed plot, this earth, this realm, this England…

William Shakespeare
Richard II

I see the coloured lilacs flame in many an ancient Oxford lane
And bright laburnum holds its bloom suspended golden in the noon.
The placid lawns I often tread are stained and carpeted with red…
"Oxford" by Tom Lovatt-Williams

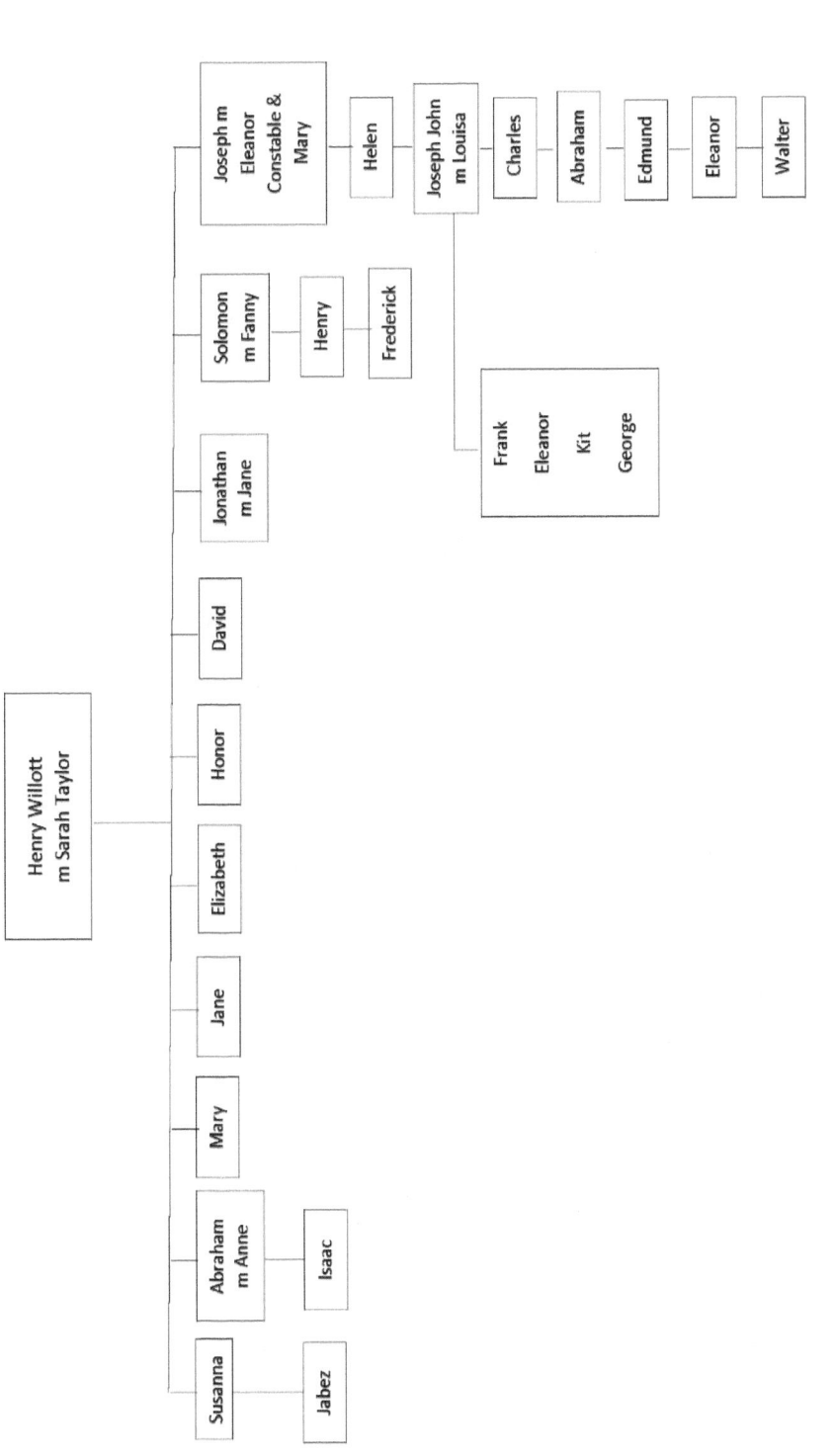

PART ONE

CHADLINGTON, OXFORDSHIRE

1802

Dawn had yet to break when Henry Willott left the sleeping household. He had waited a week already, hoping the heavy rains would subside sufficiently to give him a good start on his journey. April was a month when unsure weather could hamper his progress, but to leave it much longer would prohibit him from finding employment in the fields that lay beyond the village of Chadlington.

The beautiful corner of Oxfordshire was all that Henry had ever known. The rolling hills of the Cotswolds, rising from the meadows of the upper reaches of the Thames, gave shelter to the many stone-built villages of his boyhood. However, the time had come for him to leave. He had said goodbye to his mother Ann and father Abraham late the previous evening, explaining to them once again, that with so many mouths to feed, he would be lightening their load. Ann did not see it this way and begged Henry to stay for another harvest. Abraham knew only too well that his son wanted to make his own way in the world and gently persuaded Ann to pack some dry bread and a can of water to be ready for their son's early morning departure.

It had been hard for Henry to reach his decision to leave the village. He had worked as his father's side man and boy, along with his brothers, in the tight-knit farming community. He was barely seven years old when his father took him into the fields to work long hours keeping the birds away from the crops. Working as a bird scarer was exhausting for such a small boy, and many times he was so overcome with tiredness, that he had slipped away to curl up in the long grass at the edge of the field.

Abraham had taught him to fish when they had been able to snatch a few hours away from the constant call to work. On quiet summer days, they had slipped away to walk the few miles across open fields until they came upon the banks of the River Evenlode, where they would hide themselves deep in the bushes overhanging the waters, in the hope of a catch. Those precious moments were edged deep into Henry's thoughts as he strode out of the village.

March had been dry and very cold during the month of his birth when he had turned 25 years old. He knew then that he would be leaving his family soon after. As soon as better weather came, he had planned to make his way south in the hope of finding work along the way. He had no destination in mind; the availability of work would dictate his course.

Heavy mists rose from the damp pastures, hindering his progress. A sharp frost had frozen the ground beneath his feet, making his boots inadequate against the water that oozed between the strips of leather that had repaired his ancient footwear. Steadily he walked on as dawn broke across the valley. Passing the Tite Inn, Henry saw the bell tower of St. Nicholas Church rise up as the skies sent early morning light over Chadlington Manor, sitting majestically alongside the church, its presence dominating the village of Chadlington.

For over fifteen years, Henry had toiled in the fields and surrounding farms, his lithe, muscled body remaining lightly tanned from hours of summer work in those same fields. From dawn until dusk, he had worked to help his father feed the family. He made steady progress along the narrow pathway as the frosty ground crunched beneath him. He was a slim, youthful man, his blonde hair falling lightly over his blue eyes, striding on towards a future unknown.

By nightfall, Henry had found a barn where he slept soundly, buried deeply in the hay bales, where rats scampered back and forth. He had saved some bread for the following day, but he knew he would soon have to find his own food.

An early start the following day saw Henry leave the Forest of Wychwood behind as he travelled the open road, stopping only occasionally to rest and to find fresh water. By mid-afternoon, the frost began to thaw beneath his feet, but his shoes remained damp and uncomfortable. His pace slowed as he once again began to seek shelter for the night. As dusk fell, the figure of a young boy rose up in front of him. Henry hurried on, lengthening his stride in order to catch up with the youth.

Hearing footsteps behind him, Tobias turned to come face to face with Henry, who held out a hand in welcome. A mop of fiery red curls burst from beneath a large woven hat, under which two pale blue eyes stared intently as a large grin began to spread across the young face. Tobias grasped Henry by the arm and shook his hand, asking at the same time in which direction he was travelling and where he was making for.

Henry had no plan in mind, he told Tobias. He was simply moving on and looking for work in the fields. First, he told him, he wanted to find a suitable place to bed down for the night. Tobias hopped excitedly from one foot to the other and wrinkled his nose, as freckles danced across his face. He knew exactly where the two would spend the night and then, on the morrow, they would journey together to Crendon where his sister lived.

Tobias had walked the route many times and was familiar with all the villages where he was offered accommodation. As night fell, Henry and Tobias left the road and headed north across the damp fields that led to a small farm on the outskirts of a hamlet. Tobias pulled open the door to a woodshed and explained to Henry that he had permission from the farmer to stay inside whenever he was passing.

Fresh hay was stacked in one corner of the shed and Henry saw a previous traveller had left an imprint where he had dug himself in for the night. Without hesitation, both men threw themselves into the hay, burying their bodies for warmth as they fell into friendly conversation.

Tobias was delighted to have a travelling companion and told of his intention to visit his sister, whose husband was the blacksmith, living in the village of Crendon. He was always welcome in their tiny cottage and assured Henry that he too would be a welcome visitor. As sleep beckoned, Tobias thought fondly of his sister, whose red curls, so like his own, were faded and flecked with grey. Elizabeth had been a mother to him from the time he was born—their mother's last child. When his father had died two years prior, Tobias took on the role of the man of the house and cared constantly for his ailing mother. Ten months to the day after the death of his father, his mother died peacefully in his arms one dark and very cold night. All attempts at keeping her warm failed, as Tobias searched for more and more wood to stoke the fire daily.

The young boy had stayed on in the hovel, waiting for spring to come, until early one morning, he could wait no longer and gathered together the few belongings that were strewn about the place, closed the door behind him, and set forth.

If they walked the entirety of the following day, the pair figured they would reach the village by nightfall. Blackie and Bessie would be there, he knew. Bessie would throw her arms around her little brother and smother him in her ample bosom. Blackie would step forward from the shadows, reach for him, and throw a large black arm around his neck.

Bessie and Blackie had not been blessed with children of their own, but the blacksmith and his wife were firm favourites with the village children, who ran to them whenever their parents were busy in the fields. Bessie's meagre food supplies were always shared with others and in times of desperate need, it was Bessie to whom the villagers always turned.

Tobias soon fell into a deep sleep, his hat pulled down hard over his eyes, his wet clothes drying on his inert body. For Henry, sleep was long to come. He thought of Ann and Abraham, having to manage without his help, but knew it had to be. He wondered what would await him when he walked into the village the following day. He had been reassured by Tobias that Bessie and Blackie were always the first to welcome strangers, but it was unknown territory for him, never having travelled so far from home before.

At last, sleep overcame his troubled thoughts, as he buried himself deeper into the hay and left his worries behind, determined that all would be well and that he would find work in the village during the coming season of planting and harvest.

The following morning, with the sun high in the sky and the first glimpse of spring, Henry shook the still sleeping Tobias and brushed the hay from his hair. He had slept well and was confident they would make the village by late afternoon, if they did not linger too long at each stop.

Tobias was slow to rise and Henry shook the young boy once again, calling to him that they must be on their way. They must clear the woodshed and the outer reaches of the farm before work began in the early dawn.

They set off at a good pace, stopping only to search for fresh water. They had covered a good many miles by noon. It seemed to Henry that spring was at last on its way as grey clouds parted, allowing a weak sun to shine through. The hedgerows were alive with tight buds and new green shoots. An air of optimism swept over Henry as he brought his arm down onto the shoulders of the youth whom he had met only a few short hours before. Tobias was a lively and likeable lad with his promise of a good meal and a warm bed as soon as they reached the tiny cottage, nestled close to the village blacksmith. Elizabeth would never disappoint friends or strangers, Tobias had told him, and Henry looked forward to making her acquaintance.

Tobias talked fondly of the Oxfordshire village in which he had spent the first sixteen years of his life. He told of the summers when the harvest had failed and the long winter months with barely enough food to feed the large family. The weeks and months when cold penetrated to the bone and every stick of wood he and his brothers had found was used to keep a small fire going. Henry nodded as the boy spoke, knowing only too well how hard life was for the farm labourers who worked the fields.

In spite of the hardships, there was a lot to look forward to for Henry and Tobias. Spring and summer would bring work and merriment at harvest time when all of the villagers celebrated a good crop. Until that time, they would both spend many hours a day in the fields, rising at dawn and working until dusk fell. The work would be back-breaking and unrelenting, but the promise of new friendships sprang eternal. Henry lengthened his stride, anxious to arrive in the village before dark. Beside him, Tobias found it difficult to match the faster pace, but made every effort to keep up. For the next two hours, he struggled for breath, determined to stay at Henry's side. Henry gave not an inch as he continued the punishing pace, easily covering mile after mile until finally, he allowed the pair to rest. They were growing close and could take a short break. Breathlessly, they both sank onto a soft mound of grass.

Just as dusk fell, the pair reached the outskirts of the village. In the distance, they could see the fires burning, as flames leapt into the darkening sky. It was a welcome sight for the two weary young men.

Tobias was ahead, leading the way, anxious to reach his sister's warmth. Blackie's forge lay on the outskirts of the village and once they had pushed through the band of trees, separating the village from the road, Tobias could see smoke curling upward above the roof of the cottage.

Tobias hammered on the heavy wooden door, hammered again, until it was swung wide open with a roar from the heavy-set man that stood before them. Blackie's face broke into a large grin as he stepped forward, punching the air with a curled fist.

"Toby, boy!" he called out, hurling himself forward to clutch the shoulders of a grinning Tobias. "Bessie! Come here!" he bellowed, turning inward.

Hurried footsteps sounded across the slate floor as Bessie emerged, her once golden curls, having faded, with wisps of grey, peeking out from beneath her cap.

"What is it, Blackie?" Her tone was short and impatient. Blackie pushed Tobias forward, into Bessie's large bosom, which strained against the straps of her apron. She flung her arms open. "Toby!" she exclaimed as she drew him in ever deeper.

"Come in! Come in!" she said, and turning to Blackie, she shouted over her shoulder, "Close the door and stoke the fire with more wood."

With Blackie's arm across his shoulders, Henry moved into the room, lit by the spark of light from the fire. The night was closing in and he was grateful to be drawn into the warmth of Toby's family.

"Sit ye down, boys," Blackie motioned, as they stumbled forward and watched as Bessie disappeared into the shadows of the room.

Toby told of his meeting with Henry along the way, how they had walked the last miles together, and how he had assured Henry of a welcome at the forge. Blackie nodded at the shy young man, whose fair hair fell over his eyes, as Henry lowered his head.

CHAPTER TWO

The promise that Tobias had made to Henry on their long walk to Crendon was everything he said it would be, from the welcome both Blackie and Bessie had given him, to the work that was available to him.

Years of working beside his father had hardened Henry to the punishing schedule he was expected to keep up in the fields of Crendon. His slim, lithe body responded to the long hours of toil, and his quiet and engaging demeanour drew him close to those he worked alongside.

Days and weeks passed, bringing early summer sunshine, which warmed the bones of those who toiled daily in the fields. Henry was grateful for the warmth of the woodshed at night, where he and Toby dug themselves into the old sacking Blackie had found for them. Bessie worked small miracles every evening, feeding them all with warm stews, after Henry had trudged back to the forge and Toby laid aside the tools he used during the day while helping Blackie.

Blackie needed help in the forge. An old injury to his left arm prohibited him from any heavy lifting. Toby was a fast learner and able to turn his hand to most of the tasks Blackie could no longer undertake. He was always cheerful, whistling as he worked alongside Blackie, laughing with him, sometimes until the mirth overtook Blackie and he spluttered and coughed, holding his sides as he rocked back and forth.

As the days lengthened, there was less rest as harvest time grew ever closer and the villagers made every effort to ensure that crops would be ready for the oncoming winter. In the meantime, there was wood to be collected from the forest and stacked in the wood shed, as well as rabbits to be trapped and hung, waiting for Bessie to work her magic.

Although the work was unremitting, Henry applied himself to every task he was given and soon became a firm favourite in the village. The tight knit community became his family, for which he was thankful; he missed his own mother and father badly, having been at Abraham's side all his life. Abraham had taught him everything and he knew his father would miss his companionship.

Strangers arrived in the village to help with the cutting and threshing of the corn and Henry found himself organising a crowd of rowdy youths into a team of competent workers, instructing each hand with a newly found assertiveness, which took him by surprise.

"Well done, young Henry. Keep 'em coming," called out Flinty from the threshing shed. Flinty had overseen the harvesting in Crendon for the past forty years and was known as a hard task master, allowing no let up in the gruelling daily schedule. He was respected in the village and took it upon himself to patrol at night, ensuring the villagers remained safe and out of harm's way.

Flinty was impressed with the quiet Henry and watched him from afar, as Henry worked unaware of Flinty's shrewd eyes upon him. One day followed another until the harvesting was complete and the whole village could look forward to some revelry.

The time came, on a long summer day, when the village could finally celebrate a successful harvest. Large jugs of ale and cider were carried into the fields at noon. Trays of food followed, as weary men flung themselves to the ground, laughing and shouting, calling to those who hung back, leaning on the gates closer to the barn, to come and join them. It was a free for all and no time was lost in swallowing large amounts of ale, as jugs were readily refilled as soon as they were emptied.

Henry sat on the far side of the group, watching his fellow workers enjoy their well-deserved moments of leisure, free from the overbearing work load placed upon them every day. This was a special time of year, when everyone came together to celebrate and give thanks for a good harvest.

Henry smiled quietly to himself, remembering the many harvests he had enjoyed with Abraham in Chadlington. He was deep in thought, when he caught sight of a young woman, dipping and swaying between groups of people, a large tray of food held high above her head, on outstretched arms. She wound her way through the throngs of singing men, long dark curls covering most of her face. Lowering her tray of offerings to each man, she teased and laughed, before darting off to yet another group.

Henry had never seen anything more beautiful. His eyes followed her as she made her way back to the kitchens for another tray of food. Emerging once again into the sunlight, her dark chestnut curls bounced around her shoulders. She approached him with the offer of more food than he had seen in a long time.

Flinty approached, smirking to himself as he neared the watchful Henry.

"No good you looking in that direction, lad."

"Is she spoken for?" asked a mesmerised Henry.

"No! But she ain't for the likes o' you, so sup up and let's get more ale down us."

Shadows lengthened as the sun went down and more people arrived in the village. The fiddlers took up their positions at the side of the barn, where the doors had been flung open for free entry. Henry remained slightly apart, watching as groups of men were broken up by the village girls who wanted to dance. Soon, the village erupted into a frenzy of music and laughter, as smoke rose high into the darkening skies and the pace of the dancers quickened.

At the height of the revelry, a shadowy figure appeared from behind a clump of young trees, a whirl of chestnut hair and dark limbs leaping high into the air, as the dancers parted to allow her entry. Arms reaching out above a smiling face, she danced to the crescendo of clapping that rose in the darkness, the lightness of her body giving way to swaying motions, as she twirled and spun on tiny feet that barely touched the ground.

Other dancers fell back into the shadows, for they knew only too well that it was going to be a spectacle not to be missed. The fiddlers kept time with the dancer, her grace and beauty unmatched in the village, her body swaying to the music, until she finally lowered herself to the ground to a roar of applause from the crowd. She moved silently into the shadows once more and disappeared from whence she came.

That night, with Toby sleeping noisily by his side in the woodshed, Henry could think of nothing other than the girl who had danced so beautifully and who had wooed the crowds with her flashing smile and graceful movements, twisting her slim, brown body to keep time with the music.

The following Sunday after church, Henry sat beside Bessie beneath the low hanging branches of the large chestnut tree that marked the entrance to the village. He wanted to know more about the young woman who had danced for the crowd and shyly asked Bessie to tell him all she knew of her.

Bessie described how Sarah was a child of the village, belonging to everybody, but to no one. Sarah Taylor, she said, was born in Crendon, the youngest of ten children. Her mother worked the fields alongside the other women in the village.

Bessie told how Blackie had crafted a wooden cradle for Sarah when she was born and Bessie had taken her under her wing when Sarah's mother had left her at the side of the field, wrapped in a blanket, while she worked. Bessie reminisced about how she had fallen in love with the child who had grown into a high-spirited girl as the years passed. With a gentle smile and a far-away look in her eye, Bessie described how Sarah was as close to Bessie as she was to her own mother and spent most of her young years helping Bessie and Blackie. Sarah accompanied Bessie when she collected wood, walking for hours deep into the forest, searching for herbs and berries. Sarah was the child Bessie had never had, she said, and she loved her deeply.

Bessie also shared how Sarah was indeed a wood nymph, whose spirit would never be captured by another. In her young life, she had lived free and roamed far and wide, often to the concern of other villagers, who sent out men to look for her in the surrounding forests when nightfall approached, with still no sign of Sarah. Bessie said she calmed the animals and was often called upon to comfort the sick and the weary. Henry listened intently, as Bessie spoke of her years caring for Sarah and began to understand the wildness in the young woman.

As the weeks passed, Sarah's visits to Bessie became more frequent in the hope she might see Henry, when he returned from the fields. Often, she ran to Henry with small parcels of food and a can of water, sent by Bessie.

With winter closing in, Henry knew he loved Sarah and wanted to take her as his wife. He worked hard at trying to overcome his shyness in her presence, which only seemed to endear Sarah to him more. Sarah knew there were young women in the village anxious to be noticed by the quiet Henry, and she also knew that he was held in high esteem among the workers and that he was liked by all with whom he came in contact.

Sarah resolved to help Henry move their romance along to the next stage and she planned exactly how to do it. Taking advice from Bessie, she prepared a lunch for him each day, which she took out into the fields. The days were cold and damp, but Sarah found an opening in the thicket, which provided some shelter. It was there where Henry was able to snatch a few moments of relief from the constant call to work.

During the long winter days, when Sarah was very young, Bessie had spent many hours, close to the warmth of the stove, teaching Sarah how to sew. Over the years, Sarah's delicate stitching had repaired many a garment and her mother often called upon her to mend, darn, or re-fashion clothes for her brothers.

Putting her sewing skills to work, Sarah begged a discarded smock from Bessie that had long been cast aside by Blackie, and she began to remodel it for Henry. She wanted it to be a surprise. Her long, slim fingers worked diligently during the dark winter nights, until at last she was able to present it to Henry.

Henry conceded that Sarah was indeed a resourceful young woman, one who would make a splendid wife. In time, Henry overcame his shyness, in the certain knowledge that Sarah was devoted to him.

With some careful coaching from Blackie, Henry resolved to ask Sarah to marry him, and before his courage deserted him, he walked briskly into the fields to find Sarah.

CHAPTER THREE

The following year, as spring arrived in Crendon, Henry and Sarah were married. Early on the morning of the wedding, Bessie left the forge to walk deep into the forest to find her favourite wild flowers. Her nimble fingers would weave a coronet of willow, interlaced with wood anemones and yellow kingcup, to be placed on Sarah's head.

Moving further into the deep wood, Bessie found lily-of-the-valley, their perfumed, white bells hidden beneath dark, glossy leaves, leaning in close for protection from an ancient oak. White daisies were plentiful in the village, so Bessie moved on, looking for the magenta flower of the corncockle. Perhaps some pussy willow and catkins to complete the posy she planned for Sarah.

Back in the village, Mrs. Taylor put the finishing touches to a newly crocheted collar, to be fixed in place on the only dress Sarah possessed. A white cotton shift, the simple garment was worn only to church on Sundays, but the delicate lace would add something extra special for the occasion of Sarah's marriage.

An hour before noon, Bessie arrived at the tiny cottage, nestled in the corner of the village, with armfuls of freshly picked flowers. Excitement in the cottage had reached fever pitch and Mrs. Taylor had shooed Sarah's younger brothers out into the fields, while the women worked on Sarah's dark curls, trying to tame the unruly ringlets that refused to be trapped and pinned into place.

Bessie stepped forward to put the wreath of yellow and white flowers on Sarah's glossy curls and to place the pretty posy of white daisies and magenta corncockle into her arms, while Mrs. Taylor fussed with the new collar, making sure it sat perfectly across her daughter's shoulders.

Both women stood back to admire the bride, a satisfied smile spreading across their lined faces. "How very beautiful our Sarah is," breathed Bessie.

"Yes" replied Mrs. Taylor. "Young Henry is a very lucky man. He's quiet enough, but strong. He'll look after the girl."

The 13th century church of St. Mary the Virgin, stood on the edge of the village, past the timber-framed courthouse. Sarah walked slowly and proudly, flanked by her mother and Bessie, leading the procession of villagers, towards the heavy wooden doors of the church, where she knew Henry would be waiting for her.

Henry awaited the arrival of his bride with Toby at his side, watching as the villagers crowded into the pews. A hushed silence fell over the crowd, their whispers ceasing, as Sarah emerged from the shadows, holding tightly to Blackie's arm. The pair moved slowly up the centre aisle, Blackie grinning widely with Sarah subdued for the first time in her young life.

The vicar's voice rose up into the ancient rafters, asking each of them to repeat their marriage vows after him. Henry's response was that of a quiet, humble man, but Sarah was determined to be heard and repeated her vows in a strident voice, bringing a smile to the lips of the elderly vicar.

Henry was directed by the short, pudgy finger of the churchman, to make his sign on the open page of the register. He signed dutifully, placing an inky cross above the words:

The mark of Henry Willott.

By mid-afternoon, the spring air had cooled and wood was dragged into heaps to make fires throughout the village. When the fiddlers arrived, Sarah danced with her new husband, leading the villagers to form circles of dancers. Blackie sat beside Bessie, both deep in their own thoughts, for they knew that Henry and Sarah were to move on in the morning and would no longer be part of the village.

Flinty had approached Henry a few weeks prior, asking if he would go to Haddenham to work in the fields there. At first, Henry had been reluctant to leave Crendon, but Flinty advised he must take work wherever it was offered. There was every indication the coming summer would be a dry one and crop planting would begin in earnest, with no time to lose. Henry knew he must make the move and that evening, brought up the subject to Sarah.

Sarah did not share Henry's reluctance to leave, in spite of the fact she had been born in the village and knew no other life. Haddenham was only a short distance away and she reasoned she would be able to visit her mother, along with Blackie and Bessie, whenever she had the time.

The following morning, as soon as the sun was up, Henry and Sarah left the village to walk to Haddenham, only three miles west of Crendon. They had few belongings, so their load was light. Bessie had said her goodbyes the night before, pressing a bag of provisions into Sarah's hands—something, she said, to get them started. Bessie promised to see them soon and, with that, they headed home to Mrs. Taylor, who wept quietly as she said goodbye to her daughter and Henry, knowing they both wanted to leave early the following day, without the ordeal of more goodbyes.

The early mornings were still cold. Henry quickened the pace to keep the blood running and warm them up as they strode towards Haddenham. Sarah remained at his side, lengthening her stride to keep up with him, glancing sideways to see the determined look on Henry's face she had come to know so well.

It was a relief to know they had work waiting for them in the next village, thanks to Flinty, whose brother had sent word that he needed extra help for the season. Henry worried about work through the winter, but put his fears aside, while he concentrated on the promise of the summer work ahead of him.

Farming was in Henry's blood; he knew nothing else, nor did he want to. Abraham had taught him well, but things were changing and keeping up with new ideas was important. The long hours spent in the fields suited Henry, as he often worked alone. His very nature inured him to the hard work and back-breaking tasks that were expected of him. Working the land meant living close to nature, tending the animals and planting crops. What other life was there? With Sarah at his side, they would overcome hardships together.

On the outskirts of Haddenham, Flinty's brother appeared through the trees to welcome them to the village. Following a pathway through dense undergrowth, they came upon a tiny cottage, its door standing open, with vines growing across the small windows. Sarah looked on in despair, as Henry ducked inside of the open door. The damp and cold struck Sarah as soon as she entered and stood beneath the low ceilings. Henry's face remained expressionless, as he nodded his thanks to the man standing beside him.

Once alone in the tiny hovel, Sarah let out a groan as Henry spun around to face her. "It's alright, Sarah," assured Henry. "We can fix this place up in no time." Sarah looked and said nothing. "Right then!" Henry said, determined to brighten the mood. "Get off, Sarah, and collect wood, while I cut these vines away from the windows and let some light in."

As Sarah vanished into the woods, Henry began cutting at the vines, allowing more light into the cottage. The entering light only served to show how depressing the inside of the place was. It was clear that nobody had lived in the hovel for some time, as animals had entered the open door and made their homes in dark corners. Henry knew he must do something before Sarah arrived back with wood for the fires. Heat would undoubtedly help, but there must be something more he could do.

Walking across the dirt floor into a small room at the back of the house, he found a broom. An old wooden table, its legs chewed by visiting vermin, stood in the corner; a brown jug, its rim chipped and splattered with dirt, sat on the window sill. Henry grabbed the broom with urgency and ran to the front of the house, where he began sweeping the dead leaves towards the open door. Dust rose and settled as he swept, until the dirt floor was clear of any debris.

Henry pumped water into the old jug, cleaning it with his hands and refilling it, before he set it down at the side of the house to look for flowers. A large clump of cow parsley grew at the side of the cottage; the lacy heads on long green stems seemed just the right flower for the jug. He grabbed handfuls of lace caps and some leaves and hurried back to the front, where he placed the bouquet into the jug and carried it to the table.

By the time Sarah arrived with arms full of wood, the tiny cottage looked like home, with sunshine streaming in through the windows. Henry took the wood from her and carried it into the house, ready to lay a fire.

Sarah nodded in approval and cried when she entered the back room to see the flowers Henry had placed on the table for her. Their life together had begun. They retraced their earlier footsteps, along the path and through the undergrowth that

Henry would have to cut away with his scythe, to find their way into the centre of the village.

CHAPTER FOUR

Sarah made new friends in the village of Haddenham as she worked alongside the women folk. Her high spirits endeared all to her as they spent long hours together working in the fields. Henry worked from dawn to dusk, often chatting briefly with the small children who acted as bird scarers, making sure freshly sewn seeds remained in the fertile earth. He remembered only too well his long days in the fields and the many times he was overcome with exhaustion, when he had hidden his small body in the undergrowth, seeking a few minutes rest from his labour. Abraham had always turned a blind eye, if he had been near enough to watch young Henry slope off. He knew with little food in the boy's belly, a long day's work sapped the energy from an eight-year-old and Henry did the same thing for the little ones, tired beyond belief before the end of the day.

As the months wore on, Sarah discovered she was pregnant and made plans to return to Crendon for the day, to see her mother and Bessie. She dreaded giving birth in the winter months, when cold winds would penetrate the tiny cottage and the damp would move steadily up the walls, leaving areas of black mould.

Mrs. Taylor was overjoyed to see her daughter and to hear the news she brought with her, as they walked together out of the village towards the forge. As usual, Bessie was there to welcome them, and the three women sat together, gossiping and laughing at Sarah's stories brought fresh from Haddenham. She told of the women she had become friends with, of their lives and the hardships they endured. Their cheerfulness helped them overcome devastating losses, which both Mrs. Taylor and Bessie understood too well. They nodded in sympathy and appreciation, recalling the loss of tiny babies, too undernourished to survive, and the heartache of those stillborn babies, who were buried hurriedly by grieving relatives.

Saying goodbye to her mother and Bessie, Sarah set out for Haddenham in the early afternoon, wanting to return home before dusk. The days were getting shorter, and her burgeoning pregnancy made it difficult for her to walk too far and for too long. Anxious to arrive home before Henry came in from the fields, she hurried along the lane between the two villages.

As autumn turned into winter, Sarah found it more and more difficult to keep warm. Henry did his best to block up any small holes he found, keeping draughts from entering the cottage, as they huddled around the small fire burning in the grate. Sarah ventured out daily to find wood, going far into the forest, often waiting until the mist and fog of early morning cleared, so that she could find her way between the dense growth of tangled branches, devoid of leaves. She dragged the dead limbs of trees that towered above her, pulling and shoving until she reached the cottage.

In the early days of January, there came a loud knocking on the door of the house one evening, long after Henry and Sarah had eaten a meagre supper. Henry pulled on the old wooden door as fog swirled inwards, bringing in a blast of cold air.

"Who the heck is travelling abroad on a night like this?" he said over his shoulder to Sarah.

The old door groaned and swung open, as an apparition appeared out of the thickness of fog that hung over the cottage. There was no mistaking that hat and the hair shoved beneath it.

"Open up, for goodness sake!" Toby yelled impatiently. "A man could die out here in this weather."

Henry was beside himself with excitement.

"Toby, lad!" he said, pulling the boy inside and slamming the door closed behind him. A dark shape, held high by Toby's right arm, sat across his broad shoulders, as Toby emerged from the shadows.

"Come boy" Henry said as he urged Toby closer to the fire, providing him a place to set down the object he had been carrying. "What have you there?"

"Blackie sent it for Sarah. It's the cot he made for her when she was a baby." Toby set down the heavy wooden cradle that Blackie had fashioned years ago when Bessie had cared for Sarah, so that Mrs. Taylor might continue her work in the fields. Sarah was soon on her feet, lunging towards a wet Toby, dragging at his clothes, to relieve him of the saturated garments. Toby shook his red curls as he pulled off his hat.

"By, tis good to see ye both," he cried, as he shook Henry's hand again and again.

Sarah boiled hot water and brought a cup of broth from the kitchen area, which she placed in Toby's shaking hands.

"We'll soon have you dry and warm," comforted Sarah "Henry, stoke the fire with a bit more wood, so that Toby can dry himself. Come on now!"

Toby's visit would be a fleeting one, for he knew he must set out before dawn the next day. Blackie would be expecting him back at the forge by daybreak.

"Oh! I almost forgot. Blackie sent a rabbit," Toby said,

pulling a brown, furry, and very bedraggled dead rabbit from beneath his smock.

Sarah was delighted to have the old crib for her baby. Blackie was a master craftsman and had worked for weeks, chiselling and smoothing the white wood that appeared when he had split the elm in two, hollowing out a rest for the baby. The bark remained intact, as two blocks of wood were attached to keep the crib off of the floor. Sarah had slept soundly for many months in the crib, as Bessie rocked it back and forth.

Sarah's baby was born, late one January night, when the wind howled and the rain poured down, heavily. Soon after, Sarah looked upon her tiny daughter in awe.

"She will be called Susanna," she told Henry. Susanna was the sweetest thing Henry had ever seen, he thought, as Sarah held her close to keep her warm. Warmth flowed from mother to baby, as Susanna's eyelids closed, her sweeping dark lashes brushing her cheeks as she lapsed into a deep slumber.

For Sarah, the fight continued to keep her baby warm through the winter months, as Susanna slept soundly in the old wooden crib. Sarah missed her mother and Bessie terribly and often longed for their comfort. The weather was so bad that she did not dare venture too far from the cottage. She went only into the forest in search of firewood most mornings and longed for the spring to arrive when she would be able to walk to Crendon to visit her mother, Bessie, and her friends again.

Henry spent as much time with Sarah as he could manage, but his days remained long and arduous, while Sarah relied on her many new friends for company. As soon as the winter months passed and springtime arrived, Sarah would be back in the fields working, leaving baby Susanna with some of the older women in the village. She had loved the times she spent with Bessie and with Blackie, who carved little toys for her, which would keep her amused for hours. She was sad that

Susanna did not have a Blackie to make such things for her, but the baby seemed content and was thriving, in spite of the cold and damp atmosphere that pervaded the tiny cottage.

By the time harvest came around, Sarah had been back working in the fields throughout the late spring and summer. She cared for baby Susanna when she could, but relied heavily on the women who looked after her during the day. At six months old, Susanna was taking notice of everything around her. There had been no time for Sarah to take Susanna back to Crendon, as she had planned. Work in the fields prohibited her from taking time out from the long hours she tended the crops, but as the leaves fell from the large oaks in the forest, Sarah found herself pregnant again.

Before winter set in, Sarah was determined to walk to Crendon to see her mother and Bessie and tell them of the new arrival. As usual, both Bessie and Mrs. Taylor greeted the news with excitement, as the three women sat beneath the cover of a large beech tree, its heavy limbs outstretched, giving shelter as they chatted. The air was fresh and cold as leaves fluttered down, leaving a thick carpet of gold around the base of the tree, against which Sarah had propped herself up. The moist ground had penetrated the light fabric of her smock, as she brushed herself down, making ready to say her goodbyes to Bessie and her mother.

Sarah knew it would be months before she saw them again and their parting was always tinged with sadness, but in an effort to raise Sarah's low spirits, Bessie threw her arms around Sarah, burying her face in Sarah's dark curls.

"Take care girl" she said. Mrs. Taylor looked on and then gently nudged Sarah forward, walking with her to the edge of the lane.

Just before the birth of Sarah's second child, Henry arrived home one evening to tell her they were going to have to move on again to the next village. Sarah had grown to have a deep affection for the cottage; it was their first home and she had come to love it and to know the area of forest that lay behind the home.

Henry saw the fear rise in Sarah's eyes, at the thought of moving house so close to the time when her baby was due to be born. He rushed to reassure her.

"Sarah. We can stay on here until after the baby is born. There is no need for alarm."

"But where will we live?" Sarah's voice rose sharply.

"I said, there's no need for alarm. Extra hands are needed at the Manor and I have been asked to go. There is a cottage ready for us. Don't distress yourself."

CHAPTER FIVE

Before spring arrived the following year, Sarah gave birth to a strapping baby boy. His strong, sturdy limbs matched the strength of his lungs, as furious cries pierced the room. Punching the air with curled fists, he let the world know that he was a fighter. Henry rushed into the room to meet his son.

Sweeping the tiny boy up in his arms, he pressed his lips against the soft pink flesh of his face to whisper in his ear.

"Abraham!" Turning to Sarah, Henry said again, "Abraham! After my father." Sarah smiled, knowing how much Henry missed the father to whom he had been so close.

"Yes, Henry," she said. "Of course."

Within a few short days of Abraham's birth and in the depth of winter, Sarah and Henry packed up their few belongings and moved to the next village. The promise of long-term work and a bigger dwelling had spurred Henry to accept the offer, although the timing was particularly difficult for him and Sarah. They tramped the lane leading into Aston Sandford, a small hamlet deep in the Oxfordshire countryside, as the sun shone brightly through the trees that lined the route. Above their heads, large limbs were heavy with frost as rooks flew between the highest branches.

Henry and Sarah trudged on, Henry dragging a small wooden cart on which their meagre belongings had been stacked, Sarah following slowly behind with Abraham and Susanna.

They found their new home tucked away in the corner of the village, shrouded by large oaks, set in deep undergrowth at the side of the dwelling. A neighbouring cottage stood close by and Sarah noticed a small pile of wooden branches had been collected for them and placed close to the door at the front of the house. She was grateful to that as yet unknown neighbour, who had been so thoughtful. She said as much to Henry, as he gave the heavy door a shove and entered the tiny room. He was relieved to see the cottage was in far better repair than the one they had left, albeit, there was plenty of repair work he would need to do. There would be little time for him to work on the cottage, but Sarah and the children needed some comfort.

With a fire burning in the grate, the place soon felt like home. Sarah knew the bitter cold would penetrate the walls of the cottage, but she wrapped the children up in anything she could find, to keep them warm throughout the night.

Henry had been fortunate in finding work in Aston Sandford. He was highly thought of at the Manor and his mind had been put at rest when he was told that he was a valued worker, as he had feared many times that he would have to search for work in other villages. That would mean moving Sarah and the children at the end of every harvest.

The following morning, after Henry had left to go up to the Manor to introduce himself, Sarah's neighbour Tilly arrived on the doorstep. It was she who had gathered the firewood for Sarah and Sarah welcomed her into the tiny cottage. As Sarah pumped water to make a drink, Tilly promised to introduce her to the villagers. It was on that day that a lifelong friendship developed between Sarah and Tilly.

~

As the years passed, both women supported each other in

times of hardship and distress. There were good times, too, as each year, when harvest approached, it was Sarah and Tilly who gathered together the other women and set about organising the food and entertainment, Sarah remembering the happy days she had spent in Crendon.

Sarah acquired some chickens which she kept close to the house, well protected from roaming foxes. When Abraham grew into a fine young boy, close to seven years of age, Henry took him into the fields to work with him, just as his father had done so many years before. Abraham was a bright, sunny boy, always willing to turn his hand to anything, eager to learn all there was to know about farming. Abraham told his father that one day he would own his own farm! Henry nodded and smiled at his young son's enthusiasm.

Over the next few years, Sarah gave birth to five more children, all of them girls. Mary was the first to arrive after Abraham, followed by Jane, Sarah, Elizabeth, and then Honor. Sarah fought hard to feed her children and to keep them warm in the harsh winters, when deep snow paralysed the land, making it difficult to find wood for the fires. With so many mouths to feed, Sarah was often at her wits' end, trying to find food that would nourish her children sufficiently to keep them free from the diseases that flourished in such poor conditions. There was no escape from the desperate poverty and constant famine.

As she grew, Susanna was always on hand to help with the younger children, as were Mary and Jane. Sarah's large family was no different than most of the other families living in the small village. There was little time for play, as both boys and girls were put to work as soon as they could be of use.

Gone was the carefree girl who had danced at the harvest so many years ago, her dark curls alight in the sunlight, her brown, slim body swaying back and forth in time with the music. Sarah had mesmerised the village in those days. Premature aging, her body wracked by the onslaught of childbirth and her many pregnancies, had left her worn. Her beautiful face was lined with anxiety, her dark hair gone, to be replaced by streaks of silver.

Henry, too, had paid the price of hard work and exposure to all weathers, as he toiled in the fields for long hours. His once handsome face was deeply lined, his tired body bent over as he trudged across the fields. He provided for his family the best he could, but the wages of an agricultural labourer would not feed them all. Instead, he had to rely on snaring rabbits and anything else that presented itself in the forest that surrounded the village. Life was hard for both Henry and Sarah.

They had lived in the tiny village for some twenty years after having left Haddenham. Henry was known as a good worker, someone who could be relied upon by those people at the Manor. Sarah, meanwhile, had forged close links with the neighbour who had first collected wood for her. Tilly had become her friend and both women depended on each other to ease the difficult times in which they lived. They shared everything, Tilly replacing Sarah's beloved Bessie, who had passed away several years before.

When Solomon was born in 1818, Sarah somehow found the strength to carry on, caring for her new baby, just as she had cared for her other children. It was the life of a woman she knew, as she joined other mothers foraging for food and wood nearby.

The summers passed, moving into wet and cold winters, giving no reprieve from the struggles and hardships that Sarah and Henry faced on a daily basis. In the middle of August, before the harvest was complete that year, and on a hot and airless night, Sarah gave birth once again. Her tiny baby was weak, unlike his bigger brother Solomon, who was two years old and walking on sturdy legs, smiling and waving to all with whom he came in contact. Abraham was working in the fields with his father, and he came to see his little brother, but was disturbed when he looked at the baby's pale face and still, almost lifeless, limbs.

Sarah spent hours holding her new baby, keeping him close to her chest, wrapping her arms around him, breathing life into his small and vulnerable body. David would take every ounce of strength she possessed to nurse him. Daily, she willed him to live, as he lay still and inert in the crib. Sarah never left him for fear his next breath would be his last. She watched his tiny chest, as he gulped for air, his cries merely a whimper.

Three months passed and Davy began to thrive, thanks to Sarah's constant care and attention. She carried him everywhere she went, never leaving him for a moment. In spite of the cold air that announced the coming of winter, his little face filled out to display two rosy cheeks that had replaced the pallor of his early days. He began to take notice of everything around him, especially his brother Solomon, who tried to entertain him. Davy watched Solomon's every move, his dark eyes darting to follow his brother, wherever he went.

By early spring, Sarah could breathe a little lighter, as Davy turned into a bouncing little boy, often held tightly by his brother Sol. Sarah knew that Davy would always be special to her, for the hours she had spent urging him to live. Davy responded with huge smiles, his dark shining eyes, so like his mother's, eager in anticipation, as he pulled at her hair and caressed her cheek with his own.

There was little respite for Sarah, as Jonathan was born as soon as Davy began to walk, followed by Joseph the following year. Sarah had eleven children and loved them all desperately. Davy never left her side, pulling on her skirts as she worked around the house. Elizabeth and Honor were a constant source of support to Sarah and she could not have managed without them, while Sarah, Jane, and Mary worked in the fields, often alongside their father and brother, Abraham.

When Joseph was born, eighteen months after Jonathan, Sarah knew he would be her last child. He was the baby of the family and with so many bigger brothers and sisters to hold him, carry him and take him out into the fields, he thrived on all of the attention he received.

Baby Joseph forged a special bond with Abraham, who was like a father to him, with Henry being too exhausted after long days in the fields to give this latest baby the attention he had given the others. Both Jonathan and Joseph clung to Sol, who became their defender and their constant companion.

Sarah fed Davy extra scraps whenever she could, found morsels of bread for him and watched over him constantly. Davy was always so thin, she thought, but he took his turn helping in the fields and around the house, taking the younger children into the forest looking for wood and finding anything he thought the family might eat. He was a quiet, shy boy, his dark eyes always alert. He missed nothing and became a solemn presence among his more robust, younger brothers.

Joseph was a three-year old toddler, firmly attached to his nine-year old brother Sol, when Sol was at home. Joseph tried valiantly to keep up with Sol and cried loudly when Sol had to return to work in the fields without him. His attention was often diverted by Jonathan and Davy and he joined in their games, waiting patiently for Sol to return.

It was a huge relief to Sarah to know that her child-bearing days were over, although she still had the task of raising the younger children. Susanna was a great help and still lived at home, working tirelessly to assist her mother with the care of the family and taking over the heavier chores her mother could no longer manage.

From early June in 1826, the sun shone down continually for three months. There was no respite from the heat, and without rain, the crops suffered badly for a second year running. Susanna approached her mother in the autumn. Sitting close to Sarah one evening, she urgently clutched her mother's hand, gripping it tightly in her own.

"What is it, Susanna?" Sarah asked her, as she saw the panic rising in her daughter's eyes. For the longest time, Susanna did not reply, searching for the right words. "Susanna!" her mother said again, at which point Susanna's head jerked upwards to face Sarah.

"I'm pregnant," she said in a tiny whisper. At 22, Susanna remained unmarried and as far as her mother knew, had no man in her life. Susanna began to weep uncontrollably, large tears falling down her cheek, as she clung to Sarah, who rocked her, until her sobs subsided.

"Susanna," Sarah said. "Do not take on so."

"But what will I do?" asked Susanna, as she tried desperately to control herself, her hair falling in lengths over her face. Sarah took her daughter's face in her hands and looked into her eyes. They were swollen and red from crying.

"Your baby will live here with the family. There is no other way." Sarah had taken full control of the situation. She hid her dismay from Susanna, at the thought of yet another mouth to feed and another baby to rear.

That night, when Sarah told Henry the news, he simply said, "Another baby will make no difference to us. All are welcome." Sarah was relieved that Henry had taken the news so well, although she knew that his gentle nature would not allow him to reject his daughter, or her child.

So, it was then, as Christmas approached, that Susanna and Sarah began preparations for the new arrival. The old crib that Blackie had made for Sarah and which had held every baby since then, was dragged out and cleaned in preparation. Joseph had been the last baby to be placed in the deep recesses of the old wooden cot, and it was soon to be used again.

Sarah hid her worries from Susanna and set about supporting her daughter, reassuring her that all would be well. Henry said nothing on the subject, but Susanna knew her father would accept her baby.

The following morning, when Susanna had left the house with Jonathan and Joseph to forage in the woods for twigs and branches for the fire, Sarah fled next door to Tilly. She needed comfort from her friend and confidante and knew that Tilly would understand her misgivings. Sarah always had Tilly's ear and she had never been more grateful when Tilly placed a large metal pan on the fire to boil water for a soothing drink.

"I don't know how I would have managed for all these years without you, Tilly," she told her friend.

"When Davy was born so frail and we didn't think he would survive that first cruel winter, you were with me, helping to breathe life into his tiny body."

"Sarah, we have helped each other," said Tilly, her kindly voice low with emotion

"How could I have coped with the loss of two of my tiny babies, both born too soon and only a year apart? Henry took each of them from my arms, to bury them in graves he and Abraham had dug. I was in the depths of despair. You came to me everyday."

The two women nodded at each other, acknowledging a deep friendship that would transcend all the daily hardships that life placed upon them.

Before the snows had left in March of the following year, Susanna went into labour. Sarah soothed her daughter, talking to her to keep her mind from focusing on the pain that was ripping apart her young body. The hours crept by and still

Susanna laboured to bring her child into the world.

Sarah knew, as every hour passed, that Susanna's labour was too long, that the child should have been birthed already, and that Susanna was becoming weaker with each minute that passed.

"Honor!" yelled Sarah. "Go next door quickly and fetch Tilly."

Tilly acted as the village midwife and had delivered most of the young children in the area. Honor stumbled out of bed, dragging garments on as she fled out the door.

"Alright, Sarah," called Tilly as she came through the door, an icy wind rushing into the cottage with her arrival.

"I'm here, I'll deal with it."

"Oh, thank goodness, Tilly." Sarah's desperation was plain to see. "She's labouring too long, Tilly. It's far too long, the baby cannot survive much longer, and Susanna, look at her, she's exhausted." Tilly bent over Susanna, placing a calming hand on her damp forehead.

"Come on now, Susanna. We can do this."

Tilly looked up to meet Sarah's eyes.

"The baby is breach, Sarah. We have to work fast. There is little time to lose."

Susanna's was not the first breach baby Tilly had delivered, but each case was different and she took stock of the situation, knowing the baby was stuck in the birth canal. Sarah knew also and glanced nervously at her daughter.

"Sarah! Hold Susanna's arm tightly while I work to turn this baby!"

Sarah spun round to take Susanna in her arms, holding her tightly, with her back towards Tilly. Expertly, Tilly manipulated the unborn child, knowing that every minute counted, as Susanna was losing the fight rapidly.

For another half hour, both women struggled to help

Susanna, until, finally, a baby boy emerged into the half light of dawn. Tilly scooped up the baby, wrapping him tightly in the rags that Sarah had found earlier, while Susanna lay motionless on the floor of the cottage. Sarah cradled her daughter's head in her hands.

"Come on, Susanna," she coaxed, but Susanna's limp body did not respond. Another anxious glance from Tilly brought her quickly across the room, holding the baby in her arms. Gently she placed him on Susanna's chest. The girl's eyes flickered, as a weak cry escaped her pale lips.

"She'll need plenty of rest," warned Tilly.

"Meanwhile, the little lad is fine. I'll come back a bit later, Sarah, so you try to get some rest, too, before the day begins."

CHAPTER SIX

Henry slowly made his way back across the fields. There was some warmth left in the autumn sun, for which he was very grateful. As he pushed on towards home, he thought to himself how harvest was over, the crops stored for the winter, and the cycle of nature complete once more.

Tilly watched anxiously from the door of her cottage as Henry approached, his stoop more pronounced than ever, his ashen face pinched with pain. He was careful to keep from Sarah those agonising moments when his body shook and he trembled with the onslaught of the agony that ripped through his chest.

Harvest had robbed him of his last remaining strength and, with each passing day, came the realisation that he could no longer carry on in the same way as he had as a younger man. Young Davy had witnessed his father's demise. His own years of ill-health had prepared him for the plight of others and he was deeply affected by the sight of his father trying to hide and overcome his increasing weakness.

Davy always positioned himself close to his father when working in the fields, a nod to Abbott was all it took, to let him know that Henry was not coping well. Abbott had known Henry since he and Sarah had entered the village with two small children so many years ago, and had always tried to ensure he was given extra rations whenever there was a generous hand-out from the Manor. Abbott and Henry had become firm friends over the years, their respect for each other growing as each season passed.

Abbott worked diligently for his masters at the Manor, overseeing the planting and harvesting each year; hiring extra hands when needed. Although Abbott was known for his fiery temper and no farm hand wanted to get on the wrong side of him, he always looked out for Henry. Over the past couple of months, he had noticed Henry's shrunken figure and the pallor of his lined face and knew the man's life was ebbing away.

Abbott allowed Davy to work close by when he put them in the fields to plant the crops, noticing the young man's devotion to his father.

Tilly was at the door as Henry passed by.

"Tell Sarah I'll see her later," she called.

It seemed that Tilly was never far away, as she sensed Sarah's unwillingness to see how ill Henry really was. She knew Henry would not see another harvest, but had kept that news from Sarah.

Sarah was waiting just inside the house as Henry pushed open the door and staggered towards the fire. Sarah grabbed hold of his thin body as he stumbled and she steered him towards his chair, close to the open fire.

Young Joseph followed his father through the door and saw immediately that Henry was gasping for breath, with Sarah bending over him, her arm curled around his shoulders. Joseph removed his father's old work boots and looking upward to his mother, he said, "Send Davy to get Abraham."

Sarah fled through the gate into the open fields, just as Tilly hurried past her into the house. Tilly's soothing words had a calming effect on Henry. His heaving chest slowed, as he took shallow gasps of air into his lungs. Joseph sat close to his father as Tilly continued her quiet murmurings to Henry, who had grown calmer and very still. Tilly stroked Henry's head, his fair hair falling over his lined face. He was old and careworn and Tilly knew that hard work and the fight against poverty had drained the life from her friend's husband, as it did so many people. At 63 years old, he was an old, old man, she thought, as she brushed the hair from his eyes and fed him a spoonful of hot broth she had brought with her.

Joseph watched as the life slowly ebbed from his father's body. Henry grew still, and his eyes closed, with a more peaceful look upon his once handsome face.

"He's gone," Tilly said gently.

Some minutes later, Abraham and Davy burst through the door with Sarah close on their heels. Tilly looked up at them and saw the colour drain from Abraham's ruddy face. He sank to his knees at the feet of his father, as Tilly stood to hold Sarah in her arms. Sarah wept unashamedly, as Davy tried to comfort her. Young Joseph, only sixteen, fled from the house to seek comfort from his sister Mary, who lived close by.

"Come home with me, Ma," begged Abraham, but Sarah refused.

Joseph and Davy needed her and she knew that soon the tiny dwelling would be filled with her daughters, their husbands, and her grandchildren.

Early the next morning, Abbott arrived with a spray of tiny pink roses he had found nestled in the hedgerow, the last remaining flowers of the season. He placed them gently in Sarah's hands and noticed how suddenly frail she looked. Her eyes, usually so full of sparkle, had lost the quality he had always admired in her.

"What will we do now, Mr. Abbott?" asked Sarah, clutching his arm.

Abbott knew that without the tiny pittance Henry earned, it

would be difficult for Sarah to keep body and soul together.

"Don't ye worry, Sarah" Abbott reassured her.

"I'll be speaking to the Manor about extra rations for ye. Have no fear."

News had travelled to reach Jonathan that same day. He was working on a farm in the next village. He and wife Jane arrived soon after Abbott left. Jane brought provisions in a basket covered with a newly laundered cloth. Jane had always liked her mother-in-law and they had spent many happy hours together, sewing and lacemaking, when time allowed.

Sarah took the basket from Jane.

"Thank you, Jane. You have always been so thoughtful. You are like another daughter to me," said Sarah, as she smiled at the young woman, standing close to Jonathan.

A few days later, Henry was laid to rest beneath a large Yew tree, that spread its dark green branches across the churchyard of St. Michael's and All Angels. The tiny church was packed with villagers, some having travelled from nearby farms to pay their respects to Henry.

For Sarah, it was the end of her life as she knew it. Henry had been her constant companion through all the hard times. They had worked together to raise a large family in the small community they had called home for over thirty years. That same community had come together to support Sarah in her hour of need.

Tilly sat at the back of the church with her husband and family, gazing at the backs of Sarah and Henry's children, their heads bowed to remember the father who had taught the boys all he knew about farming and had encouraged the girls to support their mother. They were a close-knit family, depending on one another for a helping hand whenever necessary. Abraham, as the eldest son, had always been a father figure to the younger children, often taking them under his wing, supervising them as they worked with him in the fields for hours each day, regardless of weather conditions.

Abraham had taken on his own small farm in a neighbouring village and Sarah was reminded of the time he had told his father that one day he would own a farm. He was true to his word, and with his wife and two young sons, he supplied milk to everybody within the vicinity of the farm. Abraham's wife, Ann, ran the dairy, with the help of their son, Isaac. She was a cheerful, ruddy faced woman, who had a smile for everyone. Her bright demeanour was infectious, so much so, that her neighbours stood to chat for a while each morning when they came to the dairy for fresh milk.

Abraham was a shrewd business man, as well as a diligent farmer. The coins his wife took in from the dairy were carefully sorted away, until he had enough money to buy another half acre of land. His family wanted for little, as his wife ensured her kitchen garden produced enough food to feed her husband and two sons.

Abraham made a weekly journey back to Aston Sandford with provisions for the family and was always greeted warmly by his mother. Abraham was an ambitious farmer and had set his sights on owning as much land as he could possibly accumulate. When he had told his parents of this plan, Henry had shaken his head, not understanding where his son had come by such adventurous and lofty ideas.

Abraham smiled and nodded at his father, knowing exactly how his future would pan out and how he would acquire adjoining land as it became available to him. Nothing in his household was wasted; the family would be self-sufficient and every coin would count. It was as simple as that.

After the death of his father, Joseph felt lost without the daily instructions from Henry. Joseph continued to work hard in the fields alongside Davy, but escaped when he could to be with his brother Sol. Joseph was restless and began spending more time with Abraham, who talked to him about new farming methods and ideas for increased productivity. Joseph was enthralled with the newfound knowledge his brother had acquired and was eager to know more, his young brain absorbing the facts and figures Abraham taught him. Joseph was immensely proud of Abraham and wanted to know every single plan that his big brother was considering. Together they spent many hours discussing the ambitious plans with which Abraham was forging ahead. His accumulation of land was inspirational to Joseph and it seemed that each time he paid a visit to Abraham, there was another field under cultivation, or an additional pasture with more cows.

Abraham taught Joseph and Sol that the world outside the village was changing. There was talk of new railways, which would move goods across the country.

"Do you boys understand what that means?" Abraham asked urgently one day, as the trio stood together in the dairy.

"It means a link between cities, and easy access into London. It will open up the country as never before."

Both Joseph and Solomon listened carefully as Abraham relayed to them all he had heard. His message was clear: "Learn as much as you can. Speak with anybody who can bring you knowledge of these events that will change our way of life."

Solomon and Joseph were anxious to embrace all that was new and were keen to find anybody who would talk to them about the changes that were ahead. They wanted to know more about these railways that would criss-cross the country, carrying goods to markets far beyond their own villages. Joseph found an ally in Sol, who began to sound more like Abraham everyday. His ambition grew, as did Abraham's, but Sol set his sights on London.

"London!" yelled Joseph, late one evening, as they strolled the lanes on their way home from Abraham's farm.

"Why not?" replied Sol.

"Abraham was always determined to own his own farm one day. Hey, he even told Pa that when he was very small, and he's done it! He found a way to make the money to buy land. More and more people are buying milk from his dairy every day. When the time is right, you and me, we'll go to London."

Sol was emphatic and Joseph saw the same conviction in Sol he had seen in Abraham—a strong determination to succeed against all the odds, to put years of poverty behind them.

"We can do it, Joe! You and me together. We can do it. You see if we don't."

Joseph punched the air.

"You bet we'll do it!" he exclaimed. Sol took a stern line and warned, "No rushing into this, Joe. Remember what Abraham has always taught us. Careful, slow planning is the answer. Nothing left to chance. It will be a while yet before we can put our plans into action, so you must be patient. In the meantime, we have to support Ma and work steadily towards the time when we can leave."

Abraham had already told them, "When you boys are ready to leave, Ma can come here and live with us at the farm. I don't want her on her own, but say nothing to her at the moment of your plans."

Content to let things run their course, both Sol and Joseph continued to work in the fields alongside Davy, being careful not to let anyone, other than Abraham, know of their plans.

CHAPTER SEVEN

Davy sat at his mother's side, always so attentive to her since the death of his father some ten years prior. Sarah always welcomed her son's company, often being able to sit in companiable silence. Davy knew of Sarah's loneliness, although she never spoke of it to him, but he saw in her eyes the shadow of sadness that passed across her face when she was unaware of him watching her.

Davy had always been special to Sarah. Ever since his birth, she had concerned herself with his health, often nursing him through the long nights when he fought for breath, his body frail and ailing, until he was well enough again to work alongside his more robust brothers.

Susanna's son Jabez was a constant visitor to his grandmother's tiny home, for he had spent the first ten years of his life living with his grandparents. When his mother married and set up home with her new husband, Jabez went to live with Susanna, but his early years often drew him back to Sarah.

Spring had arrived early and Jabez was anxious to visit Sarah and Davy. He walked briskly between the hawthorn bushes on either side of the narrow lane, his long legs powering him forward as he strode on. Recently he had spent more time in the company of his Uncle Davy, who spoke to him of world affairs and of a world far beyond the cluster of small Oxfordshire villages in which they lived. Davy had told him of new lands on the other side of the world, lands that held promise and riches beyond their wildest dreams.

Jabez had only ever known life within his own small farming community. Davy, however, spoke to him of things he heard whilst swilling ale in the local inn with other farm hands. Stories abounded of the richness of these far-off lands and Davy was eager to share this news with Jabez.

Jabez was in awe of Davy, for he knew things that others didn't. So willing was Davy, to impart his new-found knowledge to Jabez, that they spent many hours together talking of another life, free from the grinding poverty that faced them daily.

Davy and Jabez were careful not to talk in Sarah's presence. Davy had warned his nephew often that his grandma must not know of such things, and he had cautioned his young nephew that she must not be concerned with worldly affairs. His mother would fret, he knew, as she had enough to worry about without hearing tales of distant lands that she would be unable to comprehend.

"Jabez!" Sarah welcomed her oldest grandchild, stretching out her hands towards the boy.

"Come! Talk to your Uncle Davy while I boil water for a hot drink." Sarah rose from her chair and went outside to pump water.

"Davy! I must talk to ye, away from Grandma," Jabez said urgently. "There are things we must discuss and quick." A puzzled look shot across Davy's lean face, just as Sarah re-entered the room. Jabez's finger flew to his lips, cautioning Davy against saying a word.

"Well, Jabez. How is your mother? Do you bring news of her?" asked Sarah.

"Oh, yes," replied Jabez, in a jaunty voice. "Ma is well, Grandma, and she says she will be here to see you tomorrow." Sarah was satisfied, a pleasing smile lighting up her face.

Davy sat on a tree stump at the back of the house.

"Well, come on then, young Jabez. What is so urgent that you must talk to me about?" Davy pressed.

"I've heard things. Things about those far-off lands you keep talkin' about," Jabez began. He paused, then continued, "I was talkin' to somebody from Wycombe who was passing through the village a day ago. He reckons there was a meetin' that drew large crowds of people." Jabez gulped air and carried on.

"Some gent, a smart dresser, they said he was, talked for a long time about life in those countries you know about."

Davy's interest was piqued, and he listened carefully. "Who was he?" he asked. "And how does he know so much about those lands?"

"Dunno," Jabez replied.

"But the stranger I spoke to said he certainly seemed to know what he was talkin' about. He reckons there's a way of gettin' to these places, all paid for!" Jabez was in full flow, and Davy listened with rapt attention.

"I drank ale with the stranger and he says he's goin' to Australia and this smart man is gonna help him get there. You interested, Davy?"

"What, interested in goin' to Australia?" Davy asked in astonishment.

"Don't know about that. It's one thing talkin' about these lands, but another thing goin' there." Davy stood up, and thinking fast, said, "I can't leave Ma." His brain began ticking over, trying to process all that young Jabez had told him.

"Davy! Grandma's got plenty of others to look after her. You've always talked about the riches these lands have to offer." Jabez could not believe that Davy was questioning the opportunity that had been presented to them.

"Well," expanded Davy, "I would have to listen to this man himself, talking about the opportunities and how he proposes to make it possible for us to get there. I can't believe it!" Davy concluded.

"There's another meetin' next week in Wycombe," Jabez told him. "Will ye come?"

Davy walked away and called over his shoulder, "I'll think about it," as he walked back towards home.

Jabez was struck with disappointment at Davy's response. So sure was he that Davy, after talking for so long about the opportunities these distant lands offered, would be as enthralled with the news as he was. His excitement had been palpable, and he felt let down by the one person whom he thought would share his joy at the prospect of such an adventure.

His mind was made up; however, he was going to the meeting the following week and he would talk with the representative he had been told about. With or without Davy, he was set for that adventure.

The following Sunday, Davy and Jabez set out for the town of High Wycombe. They left in the early morning, just as the larks were rising, the wet ground squelching beneath their boots. Spring had not warmed the earth yet and the deep tracks left by heavy wagons had filled with water overnight. After the first two miles, they slipped between the hedgerows into the fields and set off again on land that was ready for planting. The two men made for a well-worn pathway at the edge of the field that would carry them on towards Wycombe. They held the church spire in their sights and walked at a stead pace.

"You had a change of heart then?" Jabez said, shooting a sideways glance at Davy, as they came onto the footpath.

"Well, I'm happy to hear what this fella has to say for himself," Davy replied.

"If it's all this man says it is, then I'm all for it," Jabez said confidently.

"Let's just wait and see what he has to say. It's a big decision, Jab, not to be taken lightly, ye know. After all, it means leaving everything behind us, including Ma and the family, and starting out on our own."

Davy's head was bent forward, and he remained deep in thought for the next few miles. Jabez started again, "I was talking to Aunt Jane the other day when she brought rations for Grandma."

"Oh?" Davy's head shot up at the mention of Jonathan's wife. He knew Jane came regularly to visit his mother and was always grateful to her for the way she cared for her mother-in-law. Jane shared her weekly baking with Sarah and often picked cowslips from the hedgerows on her way into the village to give to Sarah, who loved the delicate blooms.

"Yeh! I told her we were goin' to the meetin' today. She seemed interested and said she would tell Jon. Then she said, 'Huh! If Jon thought he could farm his own land, well, he'd go to the end of the earth to do it. I know my husband.' I laughed and said to her, 'Australia is the end of the earth!'"

The sun rose higher in the sky as both men made steady progress until they came within the town's limits. Davy had been once before to Wycombe when Mr. Abbott had ordered him up atop the hay cart to secure the load and then to ride beside him on the journey. It had been a huge thrill, for it was the first time Davy had been outside the ring of small villages that were home to him. His stride lengthened, in anticipation of once again seeing those big, old buildings that had mesmerised him on that previous visit. He and Abbott, Davy recalled, wandered into the Antelope public house, where Mr.

Abbott had bought him ale and then shown him the sights. They had walked to the Guildhall, with its open arcade on the ground floor, across to the corn market in the centre of town, facing onto Church Square. Oh! The thrill of it all, Davy remembered. The hustle and bustle of the town had both alarmed and excited him. The cries of stall holders rose above the grunts of animals, as farmers drove swine and cattle through the narrow streets into the centre of town to the market pens.

Davy guided Jabez along the river bank of the Wye, the flowing waters leading them directly into the town. Their meeting was to be held in Church Square, at the very centre of the town. A large crowd was expected to form at noon. Davy and Jabez reached the outskirts of town well before midday and made their way into the centre. Jabez's head was flung back, as he looked upward to take in the plumb-coloured brick and slate roof of the corn market. On then to pass through the church gates, to sit a while in the shadows of the medieval Church of All Saints.

"Well, lad. We're here!" Davy chuckled, looking at Jabez. "What do ya make of it then?" he smiled.

"It's a big place and so busy everywhere," Jabez replied, looking all around him. They sat in silence, both lost in their own thoughts and dreams, until Davy's voice broke through the quiet between them.

"Let's go, Jab, it's nearly midday and we want to get a good place at the front of the crowd, so we can hear everything, eh?"

~

Ivor Jennings paced back and forth across Church Square; the midday sun struggled through grey clouds to highlight the sheen of his top hat. He held a pair of cloth gloves in his right hand, which he slapped across his thigh from time to time as he paced, pausing frequently to pull a pocket watch from his silk waistcoat.

Jennings was a stout, portly man of indeterminate age, sporting a full set of handsome whiskers. He prided himself on his dress, the care of which Mrs. Jennings took to a high degree, save she enrage her husband if he was unable to locate the pin that held his cravat in place. Jennings was not a man to adorn himself with jewellery, with the exception of his cravat pin and the heavy gold signet ring he wore on the little finger of his left hand.

The crowd was swelling, people pushing and jostling for a better position, as the church clock struck midday. His was a practiced art, keeping the crowed waiting just a little longer, so they became impatient to hear what he had to say.

A wooden dais had been erected in the centre of the square. Ivor Jennings pulled himself up to his full height and mounted the platform, as the crowd surged forward to surround him. He cleared his throat in an important manner, holding up both hands in welcome to those who had travelled to hear him speak.

Jennings had spent the last few years of his life travelling around the country, speaking to farmers, encouraging them to take the opportunities he offered, of a new life away from the grinding poverty. He could tell a good story and always held the crowd enthralled with the picture he painted of a new life in lands of milk and honey.

He told of the land that would be openly available to them. No more would they have to work for others, but that they would be free to cultivate and harvest their own crops. He warned of the harsh weather conditions and the hard work, but told of the rewards that were to be reaped. "A fresh start! A new beginning!" he boomed. All they had to do was to sign up and he would do the rest.

Ships were leaving Plymouth everyday, full of immigrants

anxious to embrace the new life he had so wondrously described. Jennings was in full flow, the crowd baying for more. They would be assisted immigrants, he explained, passage booked on a ship leaving Plymouth for Australia. It was as simple as that.

A clerk stepped forward. "Come this way!" he shouted above the noise of the crowd. "Form a line here. Keep it orderly, please."

There was a shift in the crowd, as they filed one behind the other to stand in front of the clerk.

Jabez broke away from Davy and pushed forward to join the end of the queue.

"Hey! Come back, Jab," called Davy, alarm in his voice. "Let's think about this first."

Jabez, however, had already been swept forward, and Davy's voice fell on deaf ears.

Davy threaded his way between the throng of men and women who were standing patiently, waiting to sign up for what they had been told was an 'assisted immigrant passage to Australia,' and finally reached Jabez.

"Hold on, Jab. Give yerself time to think about this," implored Davy, desperation breaking out across his pale face.

"Nothing to think about, Davy, I'm goin'," said Jabez.

"I can't do it! I can't!" Davy fell back from the line and sank to his knees on the ground. He thought of Ma, he thought of his sister Susanna. Jabez was her only child and he knew she would blame him for not taking more care with her son.

Davy walked to the edge of the crowd and waited for Jabez, dread rising in his throat. What had he done in bringing Jabez to this place? But he knew instantly that Jabez would have made his way here on his own, so determined was he to start a new life.

"Well, that's done. I'm on the Joshua, out of Plymouth!"

Jabez's words cut sharply across his thoughts, as his nephew joined him close to the churchyard gates.

"No! No, Jab!" Davy cried.

"'Tis too late now," said Jabez, his voice jubilant.

Davy's head sank in despair at the thought of young Jabez travelling to the other side of the world on his own. He couldn't let him do it alone. He needed someone to keep an eye on him. Davy's head jerked up.

"You cannot go alone, Jab. I'll come with you."

With that, Davy joined the line that snaked past the corn market and out in front of the Guildhall. Jabez walked through the churchyard gates and sat in silence beneath the towering oaks to contemplate the new life ahead of him. His thoughts held no fear, just pure excitement that washed over him when he thought of the sea voyage and the life that awaited him in Australia. Davy was at his side once again.

"I've signed," he said shortly.

"I can't get on the Joshua, but I'm booked out of Plymouth on the same day as you. We'll meet up when we get there." Jabez slapped his uncle on the back and Davy grinned at him, feeling better about the fact that he would, at least, be able to take care of Jabez in the foreign land.

CHAPTER EIGHT

There was little time for Jabez and Davy to discuss their future plans at length as crop planting was well underway. They did however, make a visit to Abraham a week after they returned from the meeting in High Wycombe.

Davy wanted to discuss the decision with his brother and was anxious that Jabez accompany him, to hear what Abraham had to say. All of the brothers relied heavily on Abraham for advice. From new farming techniques to world affairs, Abraham was the authority to whom they all listened, before making any big decisions, and travelling to Australia certainly counted as a 'big decision'.

Abraham's wife, Ann, was in the dairy with Isaac when Davy and Jabez arrived. Her sunny smile greeted them. Leaving Isaac in the dairy, she walked with them across the fields to where Abraham was working.

"Abe's just bought more land; he's in the top pasture," she explained.

"More land?" Davy could not hide his surprise.

"Yes," said Ann.

"We're now supplying the whole village and beyond with milk. Can hardly keep up with it. Thank goodness for Isaac, the lad works from dawn to dusk, what with Abe in the fields all day."

Ann pushed open the gate and led the way through into the new pasture land recently purchased by Abraham.

"Abe!" she called."Davy's here to see ye." Abraham spun round, a large grin spreading across his weather-beaten face.

"Well! Well! How are ye boys? And you Jab? Been to see ye grandma, have you?"

"Not yet, Uncle Abe. I'll call on her on the way back. We wanted to see you first."

"Oh? And how can I help?" Abraham asked.

Davy broke in, "We need some urgent advice, Abe. Can we talk to you?" Davy glanced at Ann.

"I'll be gettin' back then. Come to the house when you've finished, all of you."

Once she'd gone, Davy outlined the plan, telling Abraham of the meeting they had attended the previous Sunday in High Wycombe. He told of the promises Ivor Jennings had made to those in the crowd who were interested in seeking a new life in Australia.

"There is land a plentiful there, Abe," Davy told him.

"They'll give it to ye for free, if you'll farm it," Jabez broke in.

Abraham listened carefully, then cautioned, "Aye, well, there's no way back you know. Once that ship sails out 'o Plymouth, you're on your own."

Davy told Abraham how he was concerned for Sarah. "There's only me and Joe there now with Ma. With Sol getting married, she relies on us." The three men moved away from the gate to sit beneath the large ash tree that sheltered them from the early summer sun.

Leaning his back against the wide trunk of the tree, Abraham told them, "I've heard many things about assisted migrants. Certainly, there are opportunities to be had there, but it's a tough life, mind you. You'll need a strong stomach to survive the months at sea!"

"We're prepared for all of that, Uncle Abe" Jabez broke in, overcome with youthful exuberance.

"In that case," said Abraham, "Make sure you both stick together and look out for each other. I can't deny it's a good opportunity if you're prepared to rough it at first. You know, to get things goin'."

Davy again brought up the subject of Sarah, saying how reluctant he was to be leaving her.

"Since Pa died, she's not been the same. I know she tries hard not to let us see, but…"

"Don't you worry about Ma, Davy. I've always told her she can come here whenever she wants. She's very fond of Ann," Abraham reassured Davy.

As much as he would miss his brother and young nephew, he wanted them to take whatever opportunities were offered to those who were prepared to work hard for a better life.

"You boys go and leave the rest to me." Abraham nodded as he spoke.

"Tis not for a while yet," broke in Davy. "We have to await orders from Mr. Jennings. He makes arrangements for us to travel to Plymouth and we'll go together." Davy placed an arm around the shoulders of the boy.

"We're on different ships, but we land in Sydney on the same day. Have no fear, Uncle."

The excitement shone from Jabez's eyes, knowing he had secured clearance from Abraham. If Uncle Abe said it would be alright, then it would be. He trusted his word.

"Not a word to Ma, or Susanna," warned Davy. "Not until we receive notice from Mr. Jennings."

Abraham nodded. "Let's go to the house. Ann will have prepared something for us."

The trio left the pasture and took the long walk back to the house across the fields.

Davy stuck to the daily routine, trying hard to hide the excitement that mounted within him as each day passed. He said nothing to anybody, careful to keep his plans away from Sarah until the very last minute.

Davy was therefore very surprised when Jane, on her weekly visit to Sarah, had said she needed to speak with him. Jane's wicker basket sat on the table, packed with baked goods and some apples from the farm, all covered as usual with a white cotton cloth. Jane was meticulous.

"I can take lunch to Davy if you like," Jane said to Sarah. "Just tell me where he is," she added, keeping her voice light

"He's working close to the Manor today. You'll see him just before you get to the gates," Sarah replied.

Jane wrapped two pieces of bread in a cloth and cut a portion of cheese from the square she had brought with her. Quickly, she pulled a small linen bag from her basket and placed the lunch inside.

"I'll be off then Ma, to see Davy," she called as the door closed behind her.

Heavy rain the previous night had left the path wet and muddy. Jane skirted around the puddles, holding up her dress as she went. She and Jonathan had heard from Abraham of the meeting Davy and Jabez had attended. Careful not to disclose too much of the plans Davy and Jabez had told him, Abraham thought it only fair that Jon should be aware of the same opportunities.

Jonathan had been stunned when Abraham imparted to him how land in Australia was being allocated to migrants who were interested in farming. Jonathan had always admired his brother's ability to acquire land, at what seemed an alarming rate to him. He secretly wished he could do the same, but after many discussions with Abraham, he had never been able to raise the money to buy even half an acre of land. His dream of owning his own farm, just as Abraham did, had begun to fade, with the hopelessness of the situation.

Jane was a good wife and mother, but no matter what he did, or how hard he worked, he could never earn enough money to buy her the things she cherished. He always thought she had lofty ambitions, but he admired her taste, as she added small pieces of lace to her Sunday clothes to make them special. She was careful with the meagre amount of money he was able to give her to feed the family. She deserved more than he could provide, he thought.

Jonathan listened as Abraham told of the meetings that were being held around the country, encouraging people to take up the offer of free passage to Australia. Australia desperately needed people of all walks of life, Abraham told Jonathan. The country had a lot to offer, but it would be hard and gruelling work for the first few years, that is, if one was able to survive the months at sea, he joked. Before long, Jonathan was hooked.

"Would ye go, Jane?" he asked his wife.

"Yes!" Jane looked at Jonathan. "I knew a while ago that Davy and Jab were talking about these meetin's," she said.

"You never said anything to me," Jonathan said, his voice rising.

"I wanted you to speak to Abe first, Jon. You know how those boys are always full of ideas," Jane said to calm her husband, for he knew she was usually right.

"Always a steady hand at the helm!" he used to tell his sons when they disagreed with their mother.

"Not a word to Ma, or to Susanna," Abraham warned them both.

"They are not to know until Davy and Jab have received word from Mr. Jennings, letting them know when they are to depart for Plymouth."

Jonathan and Jane looked at each other and both nodded to Abraham. "Of course," they said. Jane, though, was concerned for Sarah.

"Oh, Abe! I've become so fond of Ma. I see her every week and I know how much she looks forward to my visits," Jane said as she wiped a tear from her eye. "How can I leave her?"

"Don't ye worry about that, Jane. I've told Davy and Jab that Ma can come here whenever she wants to," Abe said. "At the moment she won't leave Joe, but when she's ready, she'll come. In the meantime, Honor and Susanna are always with her."

Jane was reassured. She glanced at her husband as they walked through the door of the farm house. Ann was busy preparing a supper for them all. She enjoyed having company and was always pleased to see Jane.

"Sit ye down and tell me all about it," said Ann, as she carried a stack of plates to the table.

"Abe. Call Isaac from the dairy."

Jonathan listened quietly to everything Abraham had to say over supper. Abraham had known of the immigration agents who were touring the country, recruiting eager young men and their families to help populate far-away lands, but had decided long ago that it was not for him. However, he encouraged his brothers to take every opportunity offered to them, as he knew how hard-working each of them was and felt quite sure they had every chance of achieving success for themselves.

As Jane and Jonathan walked home, with Abraham's blessing on their minds, they could talk of nothing else. A new life awaited them in Australia. Jonathan would take advantage of the land being offered to new immigrants. At last, he thought, he had every chance of owning his own farm.

They made plans to seek out Mr. Jennings when he was

next in the area. They wanted their names on the shipping list and, in their minds, stood ready to leave as soon as they were given word of their departure. Meanwhile, they knew they must go on, not letting anybody else know of their plans.

CHAPTER NINE

Sarah sat close to the open fire. She should really have saved the wood she had collected for a little later in the year, but the evening was cold, despite the fact the autumn sunshine had sent warmth through the open windows earlier in the day. The thought of losing her precious son and grandson to Australia filled her with dread. She knew she had to give them her blessing, but her heart was breaking, knowing how final that long journey would be.

The apple wood burning in the grate spluttered and spat; Sarah knew it was not the best wood for fires, but it was all she had managed to collect. The gnarled old tree that stood close to the cottage had produced a bounty of bright red apples over the years, but, like herself, the life was draining out of it. Its once strong limbs were twisted with age, but still it hung on, a source of warmth for her old bones.

When Sarah and Henry had first arrived in the village, that apple tree had been a mere sapling and Sarah recalled the many hours she had sat beneath the boughs to nurse her babies. When she had been heavy with child, she sought comfort beneath the leafy branches, away from the hot summer suns.

Yes, mused Sarah, an old and faithful friend, giving shelter freely in the summer and offering up its dead branches for warmth in the winter. Its life almost spent, the winter winds took advantage of its frailty, wrenching broken limbs from the very heart of the tree that had once given so much.

Sarah thought of her family, her fine sons and her gentle daughters, all of them giving what they could of themselves to help her survive the loss of her beloved Henry. Since his death, each one of them had brought her comfort.

There came a gentle tapping on the door and before she could rise from her chair, Tilly had entered the room and was standing beside her.

"Oh, Tilly!" cried Sarah. Tilly knelt close to her old friend, placing her arms around Sarah's neck, her mouth close to Sarah's ear.

"I know! I know!" she said softly.

"Australia! Who would have thought it?" Sarah's face was pale, her eyes red with crying as she looked up at Tilly.

"Jab's young and strong, but Davy…" Her words drifted off as Tilly moved to sit in Henry's old chair.

"It'll be a good life for them, Sarah," Tilly said, not quite knowing how to comfort her friend.

"Davy's chest has always been so bad. Many a night he can't breathe." Sarah wiped her eyes again.

"Remember, Tilly, how we nursed him as a baby, night after night when we thought he'd never see the light of day again?"

Tilly nodded, remembering those long nights when she had taken turns with Sarah, walking and rocking Davy in her arms, his tiny chest heaving as he struggled to take in air.

"And now, Tilly, they'll be gone by Michaelmas," Sarah wailed. "Both of them."

Tilly sighed and looked away from Sarah.

"Davy said he didn't want Jab to go alone. He thinks he owes it to his sister to look after her son."

Sarah struggled to rise from the chair.

"Let me pump some water, Tilly, and we'll have a drink together."

Sarah was pleased to be outside to get the water; she needed to breathe and take in some air. She couldn't believe that once Davy left, there was little chance of her ever seeing him again. She had yet to face Susanna and wondered how she would be able to bring some comfort to her daughter upon losing her only son. After Susanna married, Jabez had left the warm comfort of his grandparents' home, to live with his mother and her new husband. He had spent the first eleven years of his life with Sarah and Henry and found it difficult at first to be away from Joseph and Solomon, both of whom were his constant companions.

Sarah pumped the water to fill a large ewer, which she carried into the house. Tilly immediately rose to take the water from her.

"Here, Sarah, you sit awhile, I'll make us a drink." Tilly wanted to busy herself, to be useful.

Sarah sank gratefully back into her chair, her eyes following Tilly as she moved about the room. Tilly was always such a comfort to her and Sarah knew she would need her more than ever.

Sarah tried to keep herself busy as the weeks passed, knowing the day that Davy and Jabez would leave was coming ever closer. She tended her kitchen garden, pulling and storing the remaining vegetables. Her onions had been strung and were hanging from the rafters. Delicate herbs were picked and carefully dried. Sarah's chickens roamed the yard still, strutting and clucking as they pecked at the dirt.

Davy tried his best to spend more time with his mother than he could afford. He was often overcome with guilt when he watched her struggle to come to terms with his departure.

There was so little he could say to her. Abraham had helped when he'd told Sarah that he believed the boys were making the right decision. She had promised Abraham that she would be strong for the sake of her son and her grandson, both of whom she loved very dearly.

When the day of departure arrived, Davy and Jabez left early in the morning in order to arrive in High Wycombe at the allotted time. From there they would be transported to Plymouth. Sarah had packed rations for them and bid them a tearful farewell. Susanna had been by her side, shaking uncontrollably and weeping loudly as she clung to her son. Mother and daughter watched as the two men walked out of sight and out of their lives.

The weeks that followed Davy and Jabez's departure were hard to bear. Joseph missed his brother badly. He and Sol became inseparable, and Joseph clung to Sol, spending all of his free time with his brother. Solomon's wife Fanny always made him welcome whenever he went to visit. She never complained at the number of times Joseph turned up at their door. She understood his loneliness and his need for his brother.

Jane continued to visit Sarah every week, bringing her any little treat she could find. She was always careful to never let slip that she and Jonathan were also planning to leave for Australia. The time had not yet come when Jonathan would be able to tell his mother of their plans, for they were yet to receive confirmation of their passage from Mr. Jennings.

Jane knew only too well of Sarah's anguish at losing Davy and Jabez and she dreaded the time Jonathan would have to tell his mother they too would be leaving. Jane pushed such thoughts to the back of her mind.

In due course, news that their passage to Australia had been booked was received. Both Jane and Jonathan were excited at the prospect of starting a new life. Jonathan could think of nothing else, other than the land he would acquire. He had met many times with the immigration agents, all of whom had reassured him that he would be offered land—as much as he could farm—and the rest would be up to him.

As he worked long hours in the fields, he daydreamed of the land he would own in Australia—his own farm and a better life for Jane and their two sons.

Towards the end of the year, Jonathan knew it was time to tell Sarah they too would be leaving. One Sunday after church, as winter crept in, they made their way up the rutted cart track to Sarah's house. Jonathan looked around him as he walked. He thought of the many memories they had there.

He saw his father waiting by the gate as he and his brothers had arrived home after long hours in the fields. His mother in the kitchen, caring for them all, admonishing the boys at times for their rough behaviour, reminding them to 'mind their manners'. A lifetime of happy memories, in spite of the grinding poverty in which they all lived.

He had the means to make something of his life, to give his two sons a better chance in the future. With Jane by his side, he knew he would succeed. It was with this confident air that he arrived at the door of his mother's house.

"Jon!" called Sarah, when she saw him. "What are you doing here?"

Quickly she turned to embrace Jane, who hung back behind her husband.

"Come! Come!" Sarah was always so pleased to have company and loved it when her children and grandchildren came to visit. She ushered them both into the house.

"Ma," began Jonathan. "We've come with news." Jane meanwhile, sat rigidly on the small wooden stool in front of the open fire.

"Yes?" Sarah smiled at her son.

Jonathan hesitated, not knowing how to begin. He had thought so many times about just how he would have this conversation with his mother, yet he stuttered, finding it difficult to put together the words.

"Ma," Jonathan continued, "we've been offered a passage to Australia."

There, he'd said it. It was out in the open. He was not prepared for the look that shot across Sarah's face as she turned towards Jane.

"Oh, Jane! I shall miss you so much."

Jane's kindness to her, especially since Henry's death, had kept her spirits up and she looked forward to the young woman's weekly visit.

"I know, Ma," said Jane. "I will miss you, too, but this is such a wonderful opportunity for us." Jane glanced quickly at Jonathan before she carried on. "Jon will be able to farm his own land, Ma. Imagine that!"

Sarah nodded, knowing how important that had always been to her son. She knew how much he wanted to be like Abraham.

"Have you spoken to Abe?" Sarah asked.

"Yes, Ma," Jonathan replied.

"And what does he have to say about it?"

"Abe understands the situation, Ma. He knows what it means to me to own my own farm."

Sarah could see the excitement that shone from her son's eyes.

"In that case, Jon, you've got my blessing."

Sarah was shocked that Jonathan and Jane were to leave for Australia alongside Davy and Jabez, but she knew that she could not hold her sons back. She wanted them to go, free of guilt, into this new life that was on offer.

"Oh! Thank you, Ma," Jane said as she burst into tears and clung to Sarah.

"I've been so worried about telling ye of our plans." Jane was sobbing.

"Tis such a wrench to leave you and the family. We have always been so close and now…" Her voice trailed off into a whisper.

Sarah straightened herself and stood up from her chair. "Godspeed, son. Come back one day a rich man, and all the hardship and longing for ye will have been worth it." With that, Sarah bade them farewell.

When the door closed quietly behind Jonathan and Jane, Sarah sank back into her chair and closed her eyes. "Dear Lord," she prayed, "Send them safe passage."

Another son and two more grandchildren lost to her. She was devastated, but she knew she had to let them go to seek a better life than this.

CHAPTER TEN

Two years had passed since Davy and Jabez had left for Australia. Shortly after their departure, Jonathan and Jane had gone also. Not a word from any of them, in spite of talk in the town of steamships that were carrying mail from Australia and New Zealand back to Britain.

When Abraham had first told Sarah that she could expect mail from Australia, he had warned her that it took many months for letters to arrive after leaving the colony. Sarah was pleased that Abraham had insisted that his younger brothers attend the tiny school in the village. Henry had not seen the need and had told Abraham that all hands were needed in the fields, but Abraham had convinced his father that even a small amount of education would improve the prospects for his brothers.

Jonathan had been a good scholar and Sarah had been proud of his ability to read and write. As a small boy, he had worked hard at forming his letters when other children ran and played. She knew that Jane could neither read nor write, but she was certain that Jonathan would send word just as soon as he could. She had to be patient and wait, as Abraham had told her.

Abraham had foreseen the changes that were happening away from the village. He had seen young men leaving the countryside for London, where they could earn twice as much money. He had heard the young Queen Victoria's husband was making sweeping changes in London and the need for labour grew daily.

Solomon and Joseph had also been keeping themselves informed of these events and had spent many hours talking with Abraham in the farmhouse, while Ann prepared food for them all. They were frequent visitors and Ann had no complaints at all.

Solomon's wife, Fanny, had agreed to move to London, which was a great relief to her husband. Fanny knew of Solomon's ambitions; he had talked to her often after his meetings with Joseph and Abraham. She understood also that Solomon desired a better life for their two sons, who had shown little interest in farming.

"But we are a family of farmers," Solomon had said one day, when the boys had complained of the work they had to do in the fields.

"We don't want it, Pa!" both boys had shot back.

There would be no resistance from them then, Solomon thought, at the prospect of leaving the countryside for London.

Joseph felt he and Solomon had waited long enough. Sarah was becoming frailer than ever and had reluctantly agreed to leave the tiny cottage to live with Abraham and Ann. Initially, Sarah had clung to her independence, not wanting to leave her home where she had so many memories, but as time went on, she knew she could no longer stay there, especially as Joseph began talking about leaving for London.

One evening, after Joseph returned from work in the fields, he went outside to pump water for his mother and returned with an armful of wood for the fire. He put the extra logs in the open grate for Sarah to boil the water and sat down in his father's old chair.

"Ma," he said softly.

"I've been talking to Abe and Sol and I want you to know about our plans."

Sarah nodded and settled back in her chair, knowing the moment had been coming for some time.

"Sol and Fanny want to take the boys and move to London. There's so much work there and the money's good," Joseph explained.

"Once they've found rooms, I will follow, but Sol wants to go first, Ma."

Joseph shot an anxious glance at his mother and was surprised to see a gentle smile on her face.

"You boys!" she said, looking directly at him.

"I'm proud of ye all, wanting to better yourselves by looking for another way of life. Your father and I were happy here, but I see how things have changed and I see this way of life is not enough for you."

"Ma?" Joseph asked. "Will you go with Abe and Ann?"

"I will, son," said Sarah.

"I'll be lonely here without my family, but I shall be sorry to leave after so many happy years. They've been hard years, mind, but I miss Pa. Abraham and Ann will take good care of me."

Sarah was certain of that and these days she was so tired. It was an effort to bring in the wood and the thought of not having to struggle through the winter months brought her great comfort. She was very fond of her grandson Isaac, a tall quiet boy, so like his father, with a head of dark curls and of Margaret, Abraham's young daughter, a sweet girl with a round face and ruddy cheeks. Yes, she would be happy there in her last remaining years.

"With the new railway line to be extended into Wycombe, Ma, we will be able to come back and see you often."

Joseph was anxious to reassure his mother, pleased that she had accepted the situation.

"You go, son," she said. "Stay close to Sol and Fanny, though."

It made Sarah feel a lot better to know that Joseph would be in the care of his brother. She knew Solomon was a man not given to excess drink or extravagances and that Fanny was a caring soul.

The following day, Joseph walked the lanes to Solomon and Fanny's small dwelling, to tell his brother of the conversation he'd had with Sarah and to reassure him their mother was finally ready to leave her home. 'Tis time, he thought.

Solomon and Fanny left for London the following week, with reassurances to Joseph that as soon as they found suitable accommodation, they would send word for him to follow on.

Abraham pulled the cart alongside Sarah's house and walked through the door, to find his mother had packed her few belongings and was ready to leave.

"Ma?" Abraham placed an arm on her shoulders. "Ready to go?" he asked.

"Put Pa's old chair on the cart," she ordered. "I can't leave it here."

Abraham swung the old chair onto his shoulder and walked out to the cart, while Sarah took one last look around the cottage.

She broke off a sprig of honeysuckle, its scent flooding her nostrils with a perfume that brought back memories and ghosts of the past. She thought of all her eleven children who had lived and played there, and of Henry, whose quiet shyness had endeared him to her and which had calmed her youthful exuberance.

Sarah smiled to herself. She had been wild all those years

ago; the gypsy in her soul long spent, but how she had loved to dance at every harvest, when the fiddlers came into the village at Crendon.

As she readied herself to leave, Tilly was by her side. "I'll miss ye, Sarah," Tilly cried, wiping away a tear.

"You'll come to Abe's farm, won't you?" Sarah asked.

"'Course, I will," Tilly replied.

With that, Abe reappeared to help Sarah into the cart. With a crack of the whip, the wagon wheels turned slowly and the cart lumbered away from the cottage.

Sarah did not look back to see Tilly wiping away tears, as she turned into her own cottage.

PART TWO

Two years had passed since Solomon and Joseph left Aston Sandford for London. Solomon had been as good as his word and had found rooms in the fashionable district of Bloomsbury. The rents were high and Solomon had wondered how he would be able to pay for the three rooms he had found in the red-brick, three storey house.

With help from Joseph, he calculated, they would just about be able to afford it, if they were careful. He had dismissed the idea of going to the East End, where the rents were considerably cheaper.

Solomon had found work immediately. He had wandered into Covent Garden to find the fruit and vegetable market swarming with people. Porters wove their way in and out of the crowds, their trollies laden with goods. The atmosphere was electric and Solomon had never before felt the vibrancy of life that abounded in the place.

He was hired on the spot and began finding his way around the market. When Joseph arrived in London soon after him, he was hired too. Both men soon became part of the hubbub and wasted no time in getting to know their fellow porters. The wages were far higher than they had ever received for the work they did on the farms.

Remembering the advice Abraham always gave, they

saved as much money as they could. Fanny was a good manager and their sons Henry and Frederick were beginning to live the life their parents had wanted for them. Solomon had been adamant both boys went to school and he encouraged them to read and to study, with promises of a good future ahead.

Having worked on the land for so many years, Solomon and Joseph were fit and healthy, more than able to lift the heavy sacks and boxes that needed to be moved and transported around the market on a daily basis.

The work was hard, but in the eyes of Solomon and Joseph, no harder than the hours they had spent in the field and well worth the few hours less they spent in bed each night. They rose early, well before dawn, to be at the market in order to start the day's work.

There was little time for leisure and certainly no money to spare for the smallest of luxuries, but Solomon and Joseph loved nothing more than to walk the streets of Bloomsbury, marvelling at the new building which housed the British Museum. The fashionable gentlemen, alighting from horse-drawn carriages, caught their attention.

One Sunday afternoon, as they strolled through the street, just as the spring sunshine began to warm the air and the tightest of buds on the branches above started to unfurl showing new growth, Solomon looked sideways at Joseph.

"You know, Joe," he said in a quiet voice. "You and me are gonna fit ourselves out in a fancy suit. There, what do ye think of that?"

Joseph liked the idea very much, but hesitated, and before he could speak, Solomon said, "I know a tailor. I put the idea to Charlie in the market a few days ago and he told me where to find a fella by the name of John Constable. He'll do a good job for us."

Solomon's voice rose at the thought of himself and his brother, strolling the streets on a Sunday afternoon, both decked out in fancy suits, especially made for them.

"Can we afford it?" Joseph was doubtful.

"We can, yes. It'll take all our money, mind, but it's important and I think it's time we started to live like gentlemen!"

Solomon burst out laughing at the look that was spreading across Joseph's face. There was joy at the thought of the suit and also the consternation of paying for it.

"Well," said Joseph, "if you're sure we can do it."

"'Course we can. Come on, Joe. Think of it!"

With that, Solomon waltzed a few steps ahead and turned to hear Joseph laughing loudly. They both agreed that the next week they would seek out John Constable, the tailor.

Fanny was all for it when Solomon told her later what he and Joseph proposed.

"Oh! You'll look so handsome, Sol. A proper gent, eh?" laughed Fanny.

Solomon was hatching another plan, but it was a little too early as yet for him to discuss it with Joseph. *One thing at a time*, he thought to himself, as he smiled at the new idea that was forming in his mind.

He knew Joseph would be with him, which was important, because the two of them needed to work together to turn the idea he was working on into a successful business venture. Just another couple of weeks and he would discuss the plan with Joseph.

They found John Constable in a small house at the back of a courtyard on Broad Street. The door was opened to them by a young woman, whose dark curls bounced around her shoulders, touching lightly on the green silk of her bodice.

"Please come in," her voice was light, shy even, as she

lowered her eyes.

A portly man emerged from behind a closed door. His light grey suit, expertly fitted, hid the swelling of his stomach, across which hung a gold watch chain. A tape measure dangled from around his neck.

"Ah!" said John Constable. "Good afternoon, gentlemen. Please come this way."

John Constable's raised arm invited them to enter the tailoring shop. As he followed them through the door, he said, "May I introduce you to my daughter, Eleanor." His eyes swept across his daughter's face.

Eleanor smiled and moved to follow her father back into the room where rolls of worsted and silk were stacked up against the white walls. Floor to ceiling windows let in generous amounts of sunlight that shone through the leafy boughs of a sycamore tree, that stood directly behind the house.

On a long table in the corner of the room, scraps of colourful silks were piled neatly one on top of the other. In separate piles, larger pieces of velvet in all colours sat near the back of the table.

John Constable saw Joseph looking at the fabrics lying on the table and turned to him, to explain.

"My daughter," he smiled indulgently. "She fashions artificial flowers from the offcuts of the waistcoats I make for my gentlemen customers."

Joseph glanced again at Eleanor. "May I see some of the flowers you have made, while your father measures my brother for his suit?" Joseph enquired.

Eleanor left the room as John Constable moved closer to Solomon.

"Now, sir. What did you have in mind?" he asked, as Solomon began inspecting the rolls of cloth that sat nearby.

When Eleanor re-entered the room with an armful of silk flowers, Joseph caught his breath at the sight of the beautiful young girl holding her exquisite designs. Eleanor's dark curls were swept upwards and held in place by a silk bow. Her clear hazel eyes reminded him so much of his own mother; he instinctively knew this was how Sarah had looked when she first danced for his father.

He fingered the fashioned blooms carefully, stroking the dark green velvet leaves, and marvelled at the intricate designs that formed the petals of each flower. The silk was carefully woven and affixed to a long stem, giving elegance to each piece.

"You've made these yourself?" Joseph looked up into Eleanor's eyes. "Why, they are so beautiful!" he exclaimed.

"It is the fabrics that are beautiful," Eleanor smiled.

"I cannot leave the pieces on the floor to be swept up by Father. It's such a waste," she laughed, a chuckle that went straight to the heart of the young man standing next to her.

After Joseph and Solomon had left the house, Joseph realised he was impatient for the next fitting of his suit. He would always remember Eleanor, framed in the doorway leading to her father's shop, holding her beautiful blooms, so expertly crafted.

In the weeks that followed, Eleanor agreed to join Joseph on his Sunday walks with Solomon and Fanny. With both men now suitably attired, the two young couples made a dash, as they strolled through Regent's Park, past the London Zoo.

The fragrant scent of pink roses, intertwined to form an arbor, rose into the air as the four passed beneath the plaited stems and glossy leaves.

Eleanor held lightly onto Joseph's arm as they strolled alongside Solomon and Fanny. Henry and Frederick ran ahead, to stoop at the water's edge, as white swans glided elegantly close to the banks of the lake, their long necks arched upward, supporting tiny heads with orange beaks and beady eyes, ever watchful.

Fanny had become very fond of Eleanor in the few short weeks she had known her. They chatted easily together, as Eleanor watched the antics of Henry and Frederick, who ran between the couples strolling up ahead. Joseph stole sideways glances at Eleanor as they walked, delighted to be in her company once again and only too aware of the time that was ticking by, knowing that he must have her home by five o'clock. Mrs. Constable had stipulated that Eleanor was to return in time for tea.

With this in mind, Joseph paused, saying to Solomon and Fanny, "I must take Eleanor home now, otherwise she'll be late."

Ever the gentleman, Solomon paused and bent to kiss Eleanor's tiny gloved hand, saying, "I hope to see you again soon, my dear."

Fanny looked on and smiled at Eleanor, as she and Joseph took their leave.

"Oh, Joe!" Solomon called after Joseph. "I must speak with you tonight. Come and see me when ye get home."

CHAPTER TWELVE

Back in Bloomsbury later in the evening, Solomon stretched his long legs out in front of him, his eyes fixed on Joseph's enquiring face.

"'Tis like this Joe" Solomon began.

"I've been thinkin' for a long time now about you and me goin' into business."

Joe's head shot upwards, a surprised look upon his face. "What?! What sort of business?"

"Well," Solomon began, "we're never goin' ta make it if we stay in the market for the rest of our lives."

"What did you have in mind, Sol?" asked Joseph.

"What I propose is, we have a business partnership, you and me, Joe," Solomon said.

"Go on." Solomon knew he had Joseph's full attention with these words.

"Huh! You, Joe, can charm the birds off the trees," laughed Solomon. He continued, "You're gonna charm every cook in Bloomsbury and persuade her to take our fruit and veg into her kitchen," chortled Solomon. "And you can start by calling on Mrs. Biggins, who sits near you in church every Sunday."

Solomon was in full flow by this point. "You're gonna sell the produce and I'm gonna deliver it. I've made it my business to find out Mrs. Biggins is the cook for the Honorable Mr. and

Mrs. William Harvey. You know where they live." He hardly paused for breath before he began again, noticing Joseph's attentive nature. "Just think of it, Joe. You can wear that suit everyday, not just on Sundays!"

Solomon was laughing at the startled look spreading across Joseph's face. "We both know a thing or two about produce after all the years we've spent growing it! We'll supply the best, only the very best to our customers. You get the order one day. I'll deliver the next day, straight from the market. How's that, eh?" asked Solomon, driving his point home.

"That's one hell of an idea!" said Joseph.

Joseph had known for some time, that he wanted to ask Mr. Constable for Eleanor's hand in marriage, but he also knew that John Constable would never agree to his daughter marrying a penniless porter, but a business man? Now that was a different prospect all together, he mused.

"I'm with ye, Sol," shouted Joseph. "That's one hell of an idea!" Joseph said again, punching the air with a clenched fist.

There would be no opportunity for Joseph to give up his work in Covent Garden. He would have to make his rounds of the big houses in Bloomsbury, after his working day was complete, when all carts had been loaded with fresh produce and sent on their way.

A few days later, in the middle of the afternoon after leaving Covent Garden, Joseph made his way towards the large imposing residence that stood at the edge of the park, overlooking a small ornamental lake. He brushed his palms together and, taking a deep breath, he entered the area steps leading down to the servant's quarters in the basement and knocked heavily on the door.

The door swung open and a surprised Mrs. Biggins beckoned Joseph into the house, as a small figure emerged from the dark recesses of the kitchen. Mrs. Biggins called out,

"Daisy! Put the kettle on!"

Joseph waited his moment, until Mrs. Biggins had made herself comfortable in an overstuffed armchair that had seen better days.

"What would you say, Mrs. Biggins, if I told you I could provide you with the best fruit and vegetables Covent Garden has to offer?" asked Joseph, the beginning of a smile spreading across his face.

"Well, young man," Mrs. Biggins looked straight at him, her tiny eyes resting on his face.

"Can you?"

"How about I bring you a selection of produce tomorrow afternoon at this time and you can decide then if you would like to order from me on a regular basis," Joseph said, making what he considered to be a fair offer.

"Done!" said Mrs. Biggins. "Only the best, mind! I want only the best."

Joseph's ploy worked; Mrs. Biggins was won over. Solomon had been right; Joseph could charm any cook in Bloomsbury and he was going to make it his business to do so.

Every afternoon Joseph made his rounds of the finest houses in the area, promising them the very best produce London had to offer. Solomon arrived promptly the next day to deliver the orders Joseph had taken.

Solomon would pick over the fresh fruit and vegetables that came before him, choosing only the very best, never allowing a bruised apple or a blemished fruit to slip past his expert eye.

Joseph, for his part, became a welcome visitor and a favourite of all of the cooks he visited in Bloomsbury. Mrs. Biggins had passed word to her friends and neighbours that they should meet and discuss their kitchen needs with "Young Mr. Willott. Such a charming man," she had cooed.

As the weeks wore on, both Solomon and Joseph came to

the same conclusion—they could now give up working at Covent Garden and spend all their time supplying produce to the households who had become dependent on them for the fast and efficient service they provided.

Within the first year of business, the brothers had taken extra rooms in the Bloomsbury house and both had ordered another suit from Mr. Constable. The two couples delighted in their Sunday afternoon walks, venturing into Hyde Park to walk beside the Serpentine. Solomon and Fanny's sons, Henry and Frederick, joined their parents on the walks.

Both boys were good scholars and avid readers. Henry in particular loved to read the tales of Charles Dickens, whose cliffhanger stories were serialised in weekly journals. Frederick, showing great entrepreneurial skills, charged one or two elderly gentleman a few coppers to read the weekly editions to them, from the journals his father purchased for him and his brother. This news amused Solomon greatly. His son was showing great prowess, he thought, smiled to himself.

Solomon and Joseph were never tempted to overspend, in spite of the fact that money was flowing nicely into the business. Remembering Abraham's advice, every penny was accounted for and nothing was wasted.

Eleanor continued to make the most exquisite blooms, spending hours twisting and shaping the off-cuts from silk and satin fabrics that dropped to the floor in her father's shop. Joseph never failed to be amazed at Eleanor's creativity.

As Joseph held the silk flowers that Eleanor was preparing to place in the large brim of her hat, a sudden thought occurred to him.

"Eleanor" he said. "Would you allow me to take a small posy of these flowers to Mrs. Biggins?"

"Why, of course," replied Eleanor. "It would be my pleasure. After all, it was Mrs. Biggins who helped you start your business, wasn't it, by talking to the other cooks in the neighbourhood?"

Joseph smiled. Dear Eleanor

Joseph arrived in Mrs. Biggins' kitchen towards the end of the week, clutching the small delicate posy Eleanor had given him. Mrs. Biggins came to the door to welcome him as usual, brushing both hands across her large bosom, as she shook flour from between her fingers.

"Mornin', Joseph," she greeted him.

Joseph smiled and held out the flowers towards Mrs. Biggins, whose eyes widened, as she exclaimed, "For me?"

"Yes, Mrs. Biggins. A small thank you for the help you've given to me and my brother."

Mrs. Biggins fingered a few strands of hair that had escaped from beneath her cap.

"Oh! That's mighty kind of you Joseph!" she said, looking closely at the tight pink rosebuds, nestled between deep green velvet leaves. "I shall pin them to the lapel of my coat when I go to church on Sunday!"

Her delight was easy to see and gave Joseph great pleasure to know that Mrs. Biggins had been rewarded for her kindness to him.

When Joseph called on Mrs. Biggins a few days later, he was surprised to see a fair-haired young woman sitting at the long wooden table with the cook. The young woman rose from her chair when she saw him.

"Joseph, isn't it?" she enquired, in a surprisingly soft voice, as she held out her hand to him.

Tall and slim with her flaxen hair drawn back into a bun at the nape of her neck, her appearance was severe. Light blue eyes, beneath feint brows, lit her face when she smiled and

Joseph was surprised at the transformation her welcoming smile made to the austerity of her features.

"I'm Mary Weller," she volunteered. "Lady's maid to the mistress."

"I'm pleased to make your acquaintance, Miss Weller," said Joseph, as he returned her smile.

"The mistress would like to meet the young woman who made Mrs. Biggins' posy," said Mary. "She wishes to add some decoration to the upstairs rooms for Christmas," Mary explained.

Joseph was taken by surprise at Mary's request. He knew that a meeting with the mistress would please Eleanor.

"Eleanor, Miss Weller," said Joseph. "Her name is Eleanor and I will ask her to call on you at your earliest convenience." Joseph's mind was in a whirl.

Joseph thought now of Eleanor, as he strode out towards Broad Street with a spring in his step. She had become so very dear to him. The Sunday afternoon walks they took with Solomon and Fanny had given him an opportunity to get to know her so much better; he admired her genteel manner and friendliness towards Fanny, who had also fallen under her spell.

Joseph left the main road and turned into the cobbled courtyard where the Constable family home stood. He was mindful of the anticipation he felt at seeing Eleanor again and was anxious to impart to her his conversation with Mary Weller. He pulled heavily on the bell and waited.

Mrs. Constable answered the door, a rather surprised look on her face, but she welcomed Joseph into the hallway and took his hat.

"Well, Joseph," she said. "How can I help you? Another suit perhaps?" she smiled.

"No, Mrs. Constable. I've been asked by Mary Weller,

lady's maid to the Honorable Mrs. William Harvey, to make arrangements for Eleanor to call upon her. Miss Weller's mistress is interested in the floral arrangements Eleanor makes," explained Joseph.

Mrs. Constable was somewhat taken aback, but saw immediately the possibilities such a meeting could bring to her daughter. She did not hesitate and ushered Joseph forward, indicating to him that he should follow her.

"Please come into the parlour, Joseph," she said. "I will call for Eleanor."

Joseph saw from the look on Mrs. Constable's face, that she mirrored his own thoughts exactly. Once inside the room, he went on.

"May I suggest, Mrs. Constable, that Eleanor takes as many flowers and floral arrangements as she can carry when she meets with Miss Weller."

"Yes, of course, Joseph" agreed Mrs. Constable "I will accompany her on her visit to Miss Weller."

With that Joseph was left in the parlour alone, to await the arrival of Eleanor.

CHAPTER THIRTEEN

Mary had been delighted to make Eleanor's acquaintance and the two young women quickly became friends.

Eleanor received a large order for Christmas decorations and was surprised to be asked to advise the mistress on colours, designs, and placements in the house, for the festive wreaths the mistress had chosen.

Eleanor worked long into the night for the next week, fashioning bouquets of mistletoe and holly, with tiny red berries held together by large tartan bows. The dining table would be decorated with bunches of white Christmas roses, expertly entwined between branches of silver.

In the vestibule, a large bowl of seasonal fruit, made from oranges that had been dried and pierced with cloves and cinnamon sticks, would give off an aroma of rich spices, to permeate throughout the upper rooms.

Mrs. Constable escorted her daughter to the residence, where they were met by Mary Weller. Mr. Constable had insisted his wife and daughter take a horse-drawn cab and had helped to load the consignment, wishing them both good luck, as he waved them off.

Mary was overwhelmed by the intricate beauty of the floral arrangements and complimented Eleanor and Mrs. Constable on their work, as she led the way through the servants' quarters to the upper rooms, knowing her mistress would be delighted with the Christmas blooms.

Mrs. Constable and Eleanor worked speedily, careful to choose the perfect position in which to display each beautiful piece, thereby ensuring Eleanor's work could be admired from every angle.

Mary stood by to take in the transformation of the rooms and marveled at the nimble fingers and keen eye of her friend. When the mistress entered the room, her hand flew to her mouth, as a sharp intake of breath escaped her lips.

"Eleanor!" exclaimed the mistress, turning towards Eleanor. "Your work is exquisite, my dear. Everything is so very beautifully made."

Turning towards Mrs. Constable, she then said, "Mrs. Constable, your daughter is very gifted. Thank you to you both for all your hard work. I shall see to it, that you are paid immediately."

The mistress left the room and Mary smiled triumphantly at Eleanor and Mrs. Constable, as she led them back downstairs into the servants' quarters.

"Mrs. Biggins has prepared a light tea for us all," Mary beamed.

Shortly after the Christmas season was over, requests for Eleanor's floral decorations came in from all over Bloomsbury. When the Honorable Mrs. William Harvey's guests had seen the splendid displays at Christmastime, they asked that Eleanor call on them also, so impressed were they with her work.

Joseph had taken to carrying a small selection of Eleanor's flower arrangements when he called on his customers to take their orders for fruit and vegetables. Below stairs, word went out when Joseph arrived, carrying delicate sprays of spring flowers, bunches of deep purple violets, and small posies of pale pink silk roses, finely fashioned to dress and enhance the outfits of the most fashionable of ladies.

Once again, Mrs. Biggins spread the word and was rewarded on her birthday, with a special bouquet of yellow freesia, bound together on long dark green stems, with the deepest blue of spring hyacinths.

The kitchen was abuzz as Joseph opened the packages of flowers that Eleanor had prepared for him. As soon as Mary Weller heard that Joseph had arrived, she descended the stairs and entered the kitchen, followed closely by Griggs, the butler.

"Pray, Mrs. Biggins, what is going on here?" Mr. Griggs cleared his throat, as he gently pushed his way between the scullery maid and Mary Weller, to take a better look at the frenzied activity in the kitchen.

"Why, 'tis my birthday, Mr. Griggs, and this handsome young man has just presented me with the most beautiful bouquet!" said Mrs. Biggins, as she pointed to the blue and yellow blooms on the table top.

Joseph dug deep into Eleanor's packages and produced a spray of tiny white, yellow and mauve crocuses.

"Please, sir," said Joseph, as he held out the blooms. "A small gift for Mrs. Griggs."

"Mrs. Griggs will be very happy. Thank you, young man" said a grateful Griggs, imagining his wife's pleasure when he handed her the spray.

Joseph made his way back home. It would soon be spring, he thought, as he walked briskly across the park. He and Solomon were now supplying most of the big houses in Bloomsbury with fruit and vegetables and he had a burgeoning book full of orders for Eleanor's flowers.

Business was brisk, both for vegetables and for flowers and Joseph knew the time would soon come when he would have to think seriously of his future. For the moment, though, he wanted to enjoy the late afternoon sun and take in the naked beauty of Bloomsbury in winter.

CHAPTER FOURTEEN

The summer passed and through the winter months, Eleanor and Joseph often went ice skating on the Sunday afternoons they met Solomon and Fanny. Thick ice had settled on the ponds in nearby parks and the four of them joined the many people who took to the ice, their feet swiftly moving beneath them, as they twirled and spun across the chilled lake.

Eleanor held firmly onto the outstretched hands that Joseph offered as support, and together they skirted the perimeter of the lake.

Joseph knew, that very moment in the winter sunshine, that spread its dazzling light between the boughs of leafless trees, that he must take Eleanor as his wife. He had thought many times of how he would approach John Constable to ask for his daughter's hand in marriage, and he had finally decided that the time had come for him to plan for their future. There was work to be done and the next few months would be crucial in putting his plan into action.

Joseph would give himself the spring and summer of the coming year to formulate his plan. Then he would go to Solomon with his ideas for the business they had created together.

Word came from Abraham on a cold day at the end of January, that Sarah had died peacefully in her sleep. It had fallen to Abraham to tell his mother of Davy's death, as soon as the news arrived from Jonathan in Australia. Abraham had knelt before her, taking her tiny hands in his, to whisper the sad facts of Davy's demise. He told how Jonathan had written of the search he had undertaken over the years to find his brother, only to receive the shattering news one day, that Davy had perished soon after his arrival in Australia. The long journey by ship, with the meagre rations allowed on board, had weakened him considerably, and without Sarah's loving care, he succumbed to neglect and finally death.

In the days that followed the news from Jonathan, Abraham watched the steady decline of his mother. She refused to eat and would not engage in conversation. Only when Tilly arrived to comfort her did she sit up and take notice, while other times, she sank into her misery and moved ever closer to death. The years of nursing Davy had brought about a closeness between mother and son and she had been devastated when Davy agreed to go with Jabez to Australia, fearing that Davy would not look after himself properly in a foreign land. Her worst fears had sadly been realised, and news of this Sarah sank into a deep depression. Losing the will to live, she soon after died of a broken heart.

~

She would be buried beside Henry in the churchyard, under the outstretched limbs of the large Yew tree that had sheltered Henry's grave for so long. That same tree would now spread its protective arms to shelter Sarah in her final resting place.

Solomon and Joseph arrived from London to attend the funeral in the small hamlet of Aston Sandford, where villagers had assembled to show support for the family and to grieve for a woman who had given so much to village life over the years. Sarah had become a much-loved figure, always ready to offer a helping hand to folk, young and old alike.

More people arrived from Haddenham and Crendon, to crowd into the ancient building. Sarah's family sat in the first three rows, her weeping daughters, comforted by their husbands, her sons standing tall and stoic.

Tilly wept softly, a tiny figure, surrounded by her family, bereft at the loss of her dearest friend. Tilly knew that Sarah had never recovered from Davy's death and had comforted her in her last days when she made frequent trips to see Sarah at Abraham's farm, always receiving a warm welcome from Sarah's son and his wife.

~

When Joseph returned to London after Sarah's funeral, he was more determined than ever that his plan would be the cornerstone of his success. He had long discussions with Abraham during his visit, making plain to his brother that he was not ready yet to discuss the future with Solomon.

As usual, Abraham gave sound advice and encouraged Joseph to undertake the plan as soon as he was ready. He saw no reason why both brothers should not be an equal success— Joseph with the artificial flowers and Solomon with the fruit and vegetables.

As the winter months gave way to spring and summer followed, Joseph and Solomon worked long hours each day, delivering fruit and vegetable orders to all of Bloomsbury. They were breaking new territory, as Joseph introduced himself to two small hotels in the Tottenham Court Road area.

Eleanor had prepared drawings of the flower arrangements to be placed in the foyer of each hotel. As the seasons changed, so would her arrangements. Her drawings were simple but effective, giving each flower in the arrangement a special place in which to show its individual beauty.

Pale colours were applied to the drawings which enhanced the display on the heavy paper that Joseph carried furled up in his bag. The hotel management was delighted with Eleanor's work and rarely changed the colourful ideas Joseph placed before them.

Towards the end of summer and with both businesses booming, Joseph decided it was time to speak with Solomon. That evening he presented himself at the door of Solomon's rooms, tapping lightly on the wood.

"Joe!" said a surprised Solomon. "Come on in."

Fanny was sitting in a large armchair close to the mantle and rose to greet Joseph as he entered the room.

"Good evening, Fanny," said Joe. "I hope I'm not disturbing you."

Fanny smiled and nodded towards Joseph.

"Not at all, Joe," she said. "Sit down and I'll go and make tea."

"I'll get right to it, Sol," said Joseph, as Solomon stretched out in front of him and Fanny had left the room.

"Right!" Solomon smiled.

"I think you know, Sol, that I'm intending to ask John Constable for Eleanor's hand in marriage," Joseph began.

"Well, certainly," Solomon replied. "A perfect choice to my way of thinkin'," Solomon added, his grin widening.

"'Tis the business, Sol, that we need to talk about. We're expandin' rapidly and recently I've taken on more and more work for Eleanor. Her creations are very popular, you know."

Solomon nodded, not quite sure where his conversation with Joseph was headed.

"I see," said Solomon. "What are you suggestin'?"

"We need to split the business, Sol. There's room for two flourishing businesses here." Joseph was choosing his words carefully.

Solomon looked up sharply, taken by surprise at Joseph's suggestion. Joseph noticed the concern that spread across his brother's face.

"I've given the new arrangements a lot of thought, Sol, and what I suggest is this. You take on Charlie. Bring him out of Covent Garden. He's as good as family and we've known him ever since we started work in the market. Make him your right-hand man; after all, you know you can trust him."

Joseph sat back, waiting for Solomon's reaction to his long thought-out plan.

"Hmmmm," Solomon mulled Joseph's suggestion over in his mind.

"And you?" enquired Solomon.

Joseph smiled, "I want to be able to invest all my time in sellin' Eleanor's flowers. Make something of myself, before I go to see John Constable."

It was a while before Solomon spoke, but finally, he said, "You know Joe, you're absolutely right. It's time we moved these businesses on and bringing Charlie out of the Garden is a splendid idea."

Solomon could see all the possibilities that were ahead of him and Joseph. The future looked bright and there was room for expansion.

"Shake on it?" asked Joseph, holding out his hand to Solomon.

For Joseph, back in his rooms later in the evening, he took a pen and some paper and set out to cost the new operation. Dipping his nib into the black of the inkwell, his pen flew across the page, forming rows of figures which told him exactly what was required in order for him to achieve his goals in the newly proposed venture.

Joseph could see the path that lay ahead of him with clarity; his judgment was sound. There was no risk involved, he told himself. He was confident he would be able to provide for Eleanor in the way John Constable would expect of him.

CHAPTER FIFTEEN

John Constable was an amenable man and had welcomed Joseph warmly when the young man had requested a private meeting with him. It came as no surprise to him when Joseph approached him nervously to ask for his daughter's hand in marriage. He had suspected for some time that the moment was not far away.

The older man had seen Joseph's devotion to his daughter and it was not lost on him that Joseph was working long hours selling Eleanor's flowers and that the fledgling business was already flourishing under Joseph's careful control.

Joseph had arrived at the meeting with Mr. Constable, clutching a large ledger that he now opened on the table in front of his future father-in-law. John Constable peered at the columns of figures Joseph had prepared and saw the business had already exceeded the totals Joseph had carefully set for himself, in only the first quarter of the year. He nodded his approval and smiled at Joseph, holding out his hand.

"I'm impressed! You carry on like this and you'll be a wealthy man in no time."

Joseph relaxed, but said nothing, his smile expressing it all.

John Constable leaned forward and said, "May I make a suggestion, Joseph?"

"Of course, sir," Joseph replied.

"Eleanor is short of materials these days; the scraps she is able to get from me are no longer sufficient, especially as orders are mounting everyday and we have already called in her three sisters to assist in the making of the flowers."

Joseph knew Eleanor's sisters were all helping with the work load and nodded as Mr. Constable continued.

"Why not send Mrs. Constable out to search for suppliers who will be able to provide you with an array of fabrics that Eleanor will need in the coming months?"

Joseph was taken by surprise, but John Constable continued, "Mrs. Constable is a very discerning woman, Joseph, she will select the finest silks, velours, and cottons in colours that will greatly enhance Eleanor's work."

This was a splendid idea and Joseph nodded his agreement. Mr. Constable looked again at the paperwork Joseph had prepared and turning towards him, he said, "These figures show you can afford such materials and I do suggest that some of these creations should be boxed, especially when delivered to the gentry."

"Yes, sir."

Joseph's quick mind picked up on Mr. Constable's suggestions. He envisioned Eleanor's beautiful flowers, encased in long, elegant, white boxes, delivered by carriage to the ladies of Bloomsbury. Yes, that would be his next step.

Mrs. Constable was thrilled to be planning a wedding for her daughter, but she was equally as thrilled when she was asked to take a carriage the following week, to purchase a selection of silks, in accordance with the colours Eleanor would be using for the coming season.

The wedding would take place in April at St. George's Parish Church, close to the Constable home. It was to be a simple affair, as Eleanor wanted no fuss. Against her mother's protestations, Eleanor insisted the occasion be a simple one, and Joseph agreed.

The suite of rooms Joseph shared with Solomon and Fanny would not do for the newlyweds, and Joseph went in search of more suitable accommodation. In a tall, imposing, red brick building, Joseph found the perfect set of rooms where Eleanor could work, assisted by her three sisters.

Solomon and Fanny were delighted to learn the news that a wedding was planned for the coming months. Fanny took it upon herself to advise Eleanor and to assist with some of the preparations that Mrs. Constable was not able to undertake.

Mrs. Constable spent long days visiting bazaars and emporiums, selecting the finest materials and often bargaining to get the best deals possible. She was fully aware that costing was a very important part of the business and was making a name for herself among the retailers from whom she purchased.

Solomon knew that Joseph would soon be leaving the suite of rooms they shared and mulled over the possibility of buying his own house a little further out of London. Fanny was in full agreement, and although she loved living in Bloomsbury and the boys were happy at school there, the thought of owning their own home was indeed very appealing.

St. John's Wood offered the perfect location and one which was sufficiently removed from the centre of London, to allow them to purchase a modest home. The wide avenues and villa housing would provide a peaceful life away from the bustling streets of London. Solomon and Fanny made plans to move to Spring Gardens after the wedding.

When Solomon shared his news with Joseph, his young brother was, once again, taken by surprise. Solomon outlined his reasons for moving out into the suburbs. Firstly, he said, he wanted to own his own property, and Fanny was certainly in agreement with that!

Perhaps more importantly, though, Solomon told Joseph, he had seen the need to find a warehouse where he could store his produce. He had taken on a second man to help Charlie with the deliveries. Joseph knew Solomon would not trust anybody other than himself, to select the fruit and vegetables from the market. He had a good reputation with his customers and he would not risk that.

Joseph listened carefully as Solomon talked of buying a commercial property in addition to his own home. Solomon's knowledge of the property market impressed Joseph and he made a mental note to speak with him again after the wedding.

Joseph saw in Solomon the same dedication and careful planning that Abraham had talked of in the early days. He recognised the same ability in Solomon to think ahead, not expand too rapidly, and always maintain a steady pace.

As the weeks passed, Joseph became frantically busy trying desperately to keep up with the demand for Eleanor's flowers. He was becoming well known in Bloomsbury for quality work, interesting arrangements, and exquisite designs. Eleanor and her sisters were as meticulous in the crafting of grasses, ferns, and foliage as they were with the dainty flowers they produced.

Mrs. Constable's ability to find beautiful silks, the colours of which matched the tinted drawings that Eleanor produced for their clients, put Joseph way ahead of any competition in the area.

Eleanor and Mary Weller had become firm friends and Mary often joined Eleanor and Joseph on Sundays when they set out for Hyde Park. The beauty of the park, whether it be summer or winter, never failed to bring joy into their busy lives.

April was drawing near and most of the wedding arrangements were complete. Spring flowers nodded their tiny heads beneath ancient oaks, whose boughs were now heavy with new buds. Swallows were returning, harbingers of spring, symbols of success and happiness. The happy trio talked of this as they strolled along the pathways, close to the waters of the Serpentine, which had become a favourite spot in which to relax, after the long and hectic days of the work week.

CHAPTER SIXTEEN

Joseph and Eleanor were married in early spring. Eleanor's love of spring flowers was echoed in the two large arrangements of daffodils and hyacinths that stood close to the altar. Green foliage sprung from ornate urns, sweeping the floor of the church with grace and elegance.

Solomon stood beside Joseph to await the arrival of Eleanor on her father's arm. Fanny sat in the front pews with sons Henry and Frederick, who were both suitably attired, having been taken on numerous occasions to Mr. Constable for fittings of their new suits.

Joseph had insisted that Mary Weller sit with the family at the front of the church. She took her place discreetly behind Fanny, touching her on the shoulder as she knelt behind her.

The organist played softly until Eleanor entered the church with her father at her side. John Constable paused before taking his next steps, until he heard the first notes of Handel's Messiah rise up to fill the hearts and minds of everyone present. The superb acoustics of the church carried the full emotion of the piece that Eleanor had chosen specially to announce her arrival. It was fitting that Handel had written the Messiah to commemorate Easter and as Eleanor and Joseph's wedding was to take place during Easter week, it would seem an appropriate choice, Eleanor had told Joseph.

The interior of St. George's Parish Church was surprisingly simple, given the imposing columns at its entrance. yet this was exactly what Eleanor loved about her place of worship and why she had introduced Joseph to it.

As the couple emerged from the church, a peel of bells rang out in celebration of their marriage. Two young people who had come together by chance had a promising future ahead of them.

Mary Weller was one of the first people to congratulate her friend and her new husband, as the small group assembled at the front of the church. She stood close to Solomon and Fanny, smiling at a few members of both families whom she did not recognise.

Mary was also the first person to take a small gift with her, when she went to visit Joseph and Eleanor in their new home. She found the building directly behind the British Museum and mounted the staircase leading up to the top floor, where Joseph and Eleanor had a suite of rooms.

A large workroom overlooked the rear of the building, where bolts of silk, satins, and cottons were stacked neatly against the wall. A long, wooden trestle stretched the length of the room and Mary glanced at the working tools spread out on the table.

Two elegant rooms in the front of the building looked out onto a small park, where flowering cherry trees, in full blossom, lined a walkway between the soft, verdant green of the lawns. Mary thought how beautiful it was and how lucky Eleanor was to have found a husband such as Joseph. She was overwhelmed with happiness for her friend.

Solomon and Fanny called on the newlyweds a few weeks later. Solomon explained to Joseph that he had been very busy completing the legalities of the two properties he was in the process of purchasing: his home and his new warehouse.

Fanny was looking forward to the move into the suburbs and had also been very busy, planning curtains and furniture for the new house. Eleanor had been quietly working on a special arrangement for Fanny and had enquired what colour schemes Fanny had in mind. Fanny had chatted excitedly about her ideas for decorations and Eleanor had taken her lead from there. Once Solomon and Fanny had settled into St. John's Wood, she thought, she and Joseph would visit them.

To have such a large and spacious workroom made life so much easier for Eleanor and her sisters, who came daily to the house to work on the floral arrangements. With each week that passed, Joseph added more clients to the business. He was calling on additional small hotels in the Tottenham Court Road area, as news spread fast that Eleanor's ideas, sketches and floral art was the very best in the West End.

When Mrs. Constable was not out in the East End looking for exquisite fabrics, she joined her daughters in the workroom, where together they spent many happy hours working with their nimble fingers to create the beauty that Joseph would proudly deliver around the area in the days to come.

Eleanor observed the changing seasons from the upper rooms of the house. The flowering cherry trees in the park lost their blossom, as soft pink petals fell silently to the ground below. The splendid show of spring-flowering azaleas was replaced by highly scented roses in large round beds deeper in the park. Bright red geraniums lined the pathways that wound through the gardens to the iron gates at the west corner of the park.

When time allowed, Eleanor took her drawing pad and pencil into the park to sketch the unfurling flowers of summer. She noted the detail of each bobbing head, transferring the graceful lines of buds and leaves onto her pad. These sketches served to assist her sisters in the workroom to model the silk petals to be affixed to long straight stems of roses and hydrangeas and to the twisting, woody canes of yellow forsythia.

Prince Albert had created magnificent gardens at Osborne House on the Isle of Wight, where the royal family spent their holidays, and Eleanor was anxious to see prints of the designs. Joseph suggested they visit the Botanic Gardens in Kew, so that Eleanor might see the new exotic blooms that were arriving daily from overseas.

Eleanor spent many idyllic hours wandering through parks and gardens, capturing the beauty of nature on the thick vellum pad that accompanied her everywhere. Joseph escorted her whenever he could, and together they enjoyed the blissful days of summer.

By the time autumn arrived, Eleanor was heavily pregnant with their first child. Joseph was attentive and insisted she rest as much as possible, but Eleanor shrugged off his concerns and spent long days in the workroom with her sisters.

After the last leaves had fallen from the naked boughs of large English oaks in the park and Christmas had passed, Eleanor gave birth to a daughter as snow swept through the wide avenues of Bloomsbury. Both she and Joseph were mesmerised by baby Helen. Her pale blue eyes fluttered beneath a fringe of dark lashes, as she nestled at her mother's breast.

Mrs. Constable rushed to Bloomsbury to visit her first grandchild and was enchanted with the tiny bundle wrapped in Eleanor's arms.

A baby carriage was placed in the corner of the workroom where Helen slept soundly during the days when Eleanor worked at the trestle table. Eleanor recovered quickly from the birth, and after a few days, she was working as hard as ever.

Helen grew into a contented child, sitting up and taking notice of all that went on in the workroom. She loved the constant attention she received from her grandmother and her aunts.

Joseph had promised Eleanor a visit to Abraham's farm and now that spring had arrived once again, he made plans for the three of them to take the train out to High Wycombe.

Eleanor was thrilled to be travelling through the countryside and looking forward to a few days with Abraham and Ann. She knew how much it meant to Joseph to make this trip 'home,' as he still missed the days when he had roamed the hills of Oxfordshire with Solomon and Davy. Farming was in his blood, and in spite of the fact he was well on his way to becoming a successful businessman, he still yearned for the old days.

Eleanor shifted Helen on her lap and looked at Joseph.

"It'll be good to be back in the country," she said.

Joseph looked away from the window and turned towards her.

"Yes, 'tis too long since we saw Abe and Ann. Young master Isaac is running the farm now, I believe, and Abe has taken over the dairy."

Joseph paused for a moment and then added thoughtfully, "We've yet to meet Isaac's wife, Jane. I understand from Abe she's a good girl and very helpful to Ann."

Joseph thought now of Abraham's land that stretched way beyond the early boundaries of the farm. He thought of the dairy that supplied milk to the whole village and beyond and of the new farming techniques Abraham embraced, in spite of his advancing years. He was looking forward to being out in the fields with Abraham, so that his brother could bring him up to date with the very latest ideas.

Joseph determined that it was Abraham's diligence that had

brought him success, his extensive knowledge of animal husbandry, his selective breeding of livestock. In these latter years and at Ann's request, Abraham had fenced off large areas for rearing chickens. Ann ruled supreme in this area and as she had done years ago when running the dairy, quickly made a success of the new venture. Villagers coming to the farm to buy milk purchased eggs as well.

Helen was at her happiest on the farm with her uncle and aunt. She toddled everywhere with the family's black and white collie by her side. He was her protector. When she tumbled, he licked her knees, when she cried after a fall, he brushed himself against her tiny body to soothe her.

For Joseph, the nostalgia of his farming days grew within him as he walked the pastures with Abraham. Abraham pointed out old, familiar landmarks to Joseph, as memories rushed back to him. Joseph knew he would never be a 'townie,' but life in London was good. His days were full, his business was booming, his wife and daughter were beautiful. His heart swelled with pride when he thought of them.

Ann had baked fresh scones and was pouring tea when the two men arrived back at the farmhouse. Eleanor, with Helen on her lap, sat in the large armchair, with Jess curled up at their feet.

The three days with Abraham and Ann went all too quickly and soon it was time for them to say goodbye to the family. Before Joseph left, though, Abraham wanted to take him to the churchyard where their parents were buried.

Ann cut fresh flowers from her kitchen garden for the two men to take with them to place on the graves.

CHAPTER SEVENTEEN

Over the next five years, Eleanor gave birth to three sons. First came Joseph John, a robust little boy who entered the world with cries that rose above the chatter of Eleanor's delivery room. Charles and Alfred soon followed, which caused Joseph to take stock of the needs of his growing family.

With four young children, more accommodation was required within the home. Joseph rented two rooms on the lower floor to be used as a workshop and a dispatch area. The original workshop was turned into a nursery.

Eleanor returned to work soon after each birth, her vitality quickly returning as she led her sisters on to create more and more beautiful blooms.

Mary Weller's young brother George was now employed to work in the dispatching area, where he boxed the flowers and made arrangements tor delivery. George was only fifteen, but he quickly made the department his own and soon mastered the art of addressing the elegant white boxes in copperplate script, the nib of his pen pushing deeply into the black ink, thereby ensuring each box reached its destination on time.

George understood the importance of prompt deliveries to the homes of the wealthy in the area. Every boxed arrangement and small spray received the same consideration and care and was delivered with the same amount of attention.

The manufacturing workforce had also been increased and, to this end, Joseph had found a number of women who were willing to make flowers in their own homes, adding to family finances and alleviating the constant pressure on Eleanor and her sisters.

Joseph saw the need for a right-hand man, somebody who would deliver materials to the home-workers and visit them to collect the flower once sprays and wreaths had been completed, taking them back to George at the house for dispatch.

A young man living in a single room on the lower ground floor of the house proved to be Joseph's saving grace and agreed to join Joseph to assist with the delivery of materials in and around St. Giles.

This made a huge difference to Joseph, who could now devote a great deal more time to expanding the area in which he sold Eleanor's flowers. Edward Mason was grateful to Joseph for the opportunity to work alongside him and resolved to assist Joseph in every way possible.

The business was running smoothly and with all of the extra help, Joseph was able to relax a little and enjoy some time with his family. He was therefore shocked to receive an urgent message from Mrs. Constable early one Sunday morning.

A loud knocking came on the door and Joseph hurried into the hallway to find a young boy standing on the landing.

"An urgent message from Mrs. Constable, sir," the young boy said, breathing heavily, his face flushed crimson with the effort of having run as fast as possible from Broad Street.

"What is it?" enquired Joseph.

"Don't know, sir. Mrs. Constable just said to come immediately."

With that, Joseph took a coin from his pocket and sent the boy on his way, calling after him, "Tell Mrs. Constable I will take a cab and be with her very shortly."

Joseph arrived to find Mrs. Constable in a state of shock, at the news her husband had died an hour previously. A doctor had been called and the body of John Constable still lay in the parlour, awaiting removal.

Joseph gently encouraged his mother-in-law to pack a bag while they awaited the arrival of the coroner. She must return with him, he insisted. All three of Eleanor's sisters were now married and Mr. and Mrs. Constable had lived comfortably on their own for the past year, since their youngest daughter Henrietta's wedding in late December.

A coachman and his cab waited patiently at the entrance to the courtyard. Joseph placed a comforting hand under the arm of Mrs. Constable as he helped her into the Hackney-cab, whose horse stamped its feet on the cobbled roadway. Mrs. Constable, still in shock, dabbed her red and swollen eyes with a white lace handkerchief.

Eleanor ushered her husband and her mother into the large room at the front of the house, her tiny face white and pinched at the news of her father's death. It had all been so unexpected, as it was thought John Constable was a healthy man, fit indeed for his sixty-five years.

Following John Constable's funeral, Mrs. Constable packed up the house n Broad Street and moved into the home of her eldest daughter and her husband. She was grateful for the company of her grandchildren, who brought her the greatest of pleasures, even in her hours of mourning.

Joseph knew the time had come for him to look for more suitable premises for his family. Eleanor was pregnant once again and with Mrs. Constable now a permanent occupant in their home, something had to be done.

Joseph travelled to St. John's Wood to confer with Solomon. The turmoil in the family in recent months had led

Joseph to a point where he was ready to look for a commercial property and from whom would it be better to seek advice than Solomon.

Fanny greeted him in a comforting voice, "'Tis good to see you, Joe."

Joseph nodded as she took his hat and followed her into the parlour, where Solomon rose from his fireside chair.

"Joe!" said Solomon, offering his outstretched hand.

"I am so sorry to hear of Mr. Constable's death. How is Mrs. Constable?" he enquired.

Joseph took a seat as Fanny left the room to allow the two men to talk.

"Well…" Joseph paused. "It's hard for her, Sol, but the children keep her busy and she's a great help to Eleanor."

Fanny entered the room, carrying a large round tray set with a teapot, milk and sugar, and two cups and saucers.

Solomon and Joseph paused their conversation, as Fanny asked, "Would you like cake, Joe? Freshly baked today," she encouraged him.

Joseph smiled at his sister-in-law. "Thank you, Fanny, I would." She promptly returned to the kitchen.

"I'm looking for a property, Sol. We have another baby due very soon and with Mrs. Constable now living with us, there is just not enough room for us all."

Solomon stood up, his back to the hearth, and asked, "You need a factory as well as living accommodation, then? Is that what you have in mind, Joe?"

Joseph considered his brother's question for a moment and then said, "That would be ideal, Sol, if I could find something like that."

Solomon walked across the room and opened his roll top desk, rifling through piles of paper neatly clipped together.

"Ah! Here we are." Solomon pulled a folder from the

drawer, holding out the papers to Joseph.

"I receive details of commercial properties available and there might be something in here of interest to you, Joe. Have a look and let me know."

Solomon took his seat and shot a serious look at Joseph.

"I've just taken possession of a small parade of shops off the main thoroughfare," Solomon told Joseph, whose face showed the amazement he felt.

"Well done, Sol!" Joseph laughed. "Business must be good then."

Solomon looked straight at his brother. "Never bin' better, Joe."

Joseph knew that Solomon had taken on more men in recent months and that his two large warehouses were well stocked with produce, but he was surprised when Solomon added, "You know, investing in property is the way to go, Joe. I want to leave a legacy for the boys and I think this is the way to do it. Young Henry collects the rents every Saturday and keeps an accounting of the income. It's his responsibility to keep the premises tenanted. So far, he's doin' a good job."

Joseph looked at Solomon and saw in his brother, the competent business man he had become. His mind flew back to the years when they had worked the land with their father. Deep in thought, he looked up to see Solomon's sharp eyes on his face.

"I know what you're thinking, Joe," Solomon said quietly. "You're remembering all the years of hardship, when we barely had enough to eat. Life was hard then, Joe. How we struggled, but it was that struggle that gave us the will to succeed, to want something more from life."

Joseph thought back to his mother and father and the hovel in which they all lived, to the long days of back-breaking labour in the fields, for little remuneration.

"We're fortunate indeed, Sol. The world is changing and London is the place to be these days, but I still miss the country."

Joseph sighed wistfully at the memories that floated upwards to the surface of his mind every so often.

Joseph continued, making ready for his departure.

"Thanks Sol, I'll have a look at these properties and let you know if there is anything there that interests me."

With that, Joseph bade his brother farewell, his head spinning with new possibilities.

CHAPTER EIGHTEEN

Late one afternoon, after Joseph had viewed a number of properties in an attempt to find a new home for the family, he found the perfect spot in a backwater behind Albany Street, close to Regent's Park.

A large white-stucco building stood beneath a sloping grey slate roof, on the opposite side of the road as the Wesleyan Methodist Chapel. Joseph viewed the chapel from one of the upper rooms in the house and noted the warmth of the red brick façade and the large dark blue doors, through which, he decided, he would enter very soon.

The house, hidden away in a small cul-de-sac, sufficiently distant from the main thoroughfare, but still in the heart of the West End between Bloomsbury and Covent Garden, made it an ideal choice. It was there, he mused, where his children would live the life he had dreamed of as a young boy, and where he would live as his business prospered.

Joseph thought proudly of his brothers, as he often did. Abraham, who had followed his dream of owning a farm, now presiding over a hundred acres of fertile land in Oxfordshire. Jonathan, also a farmer, buying up acres of farmland in Australia, supported by his two grown sons, and of Solomon and Fanny, with Solomon having become a very successful businessman and property owner.

If only Henry and Sarah had lived to see their children prosper in such a way, he thought, as he strode between the rooms, looking at walls and ceilings, window frames and flooring. Success had come to each one of them, through sheer hard work and by overcoming and surmounting seemingly impossible difficulties. Joseph knew that what each brother lacked in education had been made up for with their smart, quick, intelligent minds.

Back on the ground floor, Joseph took one last, lingering look at the factory area. The high ceilings and large windows, allowing natural light and sunshine to penetrate, would make the working areas pleasant places to be. A thrill cut through his chest, as he envisioned a busy workroom, leading directly onto the dispatching area. Storage rooms, fitted out with shelving for the bales of cloth, delivered frequently from the East End. Racks for boxes, wrapping paper, and ribbons, which George used with great expertise, to turn into beautiful packaging ready for delivery.

Joseph realised there was a fair amount of work to be done to achieve these goals and scribbled notes for himself as he took his final walk around the premises. He had noted, whilst on the upper level, that a number of rooms running across the back of the building could be converted into bedrooms for the children, with a small nursey located at the end of the hallway. Tucked into a corner on the far side of the house, close to the staircase, was a large storage area that would provide a bedroom and sitting room for Mrs. Constable.

The large rooms at the front of the house on the upper level would be used as living accommodations for the family. The work would not be completed before Eleanor had the baby, but Joseph was anxious to have her settled as soon after the birth as possible.

Eleanor welcomed Joseph when he arrived home early in

the evening, with the news that he had found a new home for them all. She listened attentively to Joseph's description of the property, as he explained his ideas for the family and for the factory.

Joseph emphasised the fact they had far outgrown their existing home, especially since Mrs. Constable had moved in with them and that Eleanor had little room in which to work on her drawings, as all available space was taken up in the workroom below, with the making of flowers. Eleanor nodded as Joseph continued with his plans.

George, he said, struggled for space also in the dispatching area, especially with Edward Mason coming and going frequently, to collect boxes for delivery to the home workers. Joseph told Eleanor that he was very pleased with the way George and Edward worked together, since he had given over control of the entire dispatching area to George. The young man worked with enthusiasm, Joseph said, and he explained to Eleanor that he was pleased to be relieved of the burden, overseeing the orders that were being prepared for delivery.

A heap of new drawings sat on the small table at the side of Eleanor's chair.

"You've been busy, Eleanor," said Joseph, taking up one of the sheets of paper, on which Eleanor had designed a large display of summer flowers for the entryway of a new hotel to be opened in a few months time.

"Yes," replied Eleanor.

"I wanted to have them ready for you to take to The Strand. I know they're waiting to see my ideas for the foyer and for the dining areas." Eleanor held out another scroll of paper she had been working on.

"Excellent, my dear. Thank you." Joseph smiled at his wife, always willing to acknowledge her talent.

Work was soon underway at the new house. Joseph had set

an army of carpenters to work on both floors, making every effort to have the home ready for the move as soon as Eleanor was fit enough to make the necessary arrangements.

Mary came to visit Eleanor, who was now housebound in the final weeks of her pregnancy. Mary lamented the lack of leisure time allotted to her, but came to see her friend as often as she could. Mrs. Constable bustled in carrying a tray of tea

"There you are," she said, placing the tray on a small round table in front of Eleanor.

"Thank you, Mrs. Constable." Mary smiled as she spoke "Will you join us?" she asked.

"No, thank you, Mary. I want Eleanor to rest, so I'm going to prepare tea for the children," said Mrs. Constable as she left the room, closing the door quietly behind her.

A few days after Mary's visit, Eleanor went into labour. Baby Eleanor was born in the early hours of the morning, a surprise for big sister Helen, who flew to her mother's bedroom when she received the news from her father.

Eleanor's namesake was a small bundle of joy, fussed over by Mrs. Constable, who immediately took charge of the new baby, with Helen's help. Little Nell, as she was christened by the family, was a contented and happy infant, her cries answered by her adoring older sister.

Eleanor soon returned to work to prepare for the move. There was so much to do with Joseph out all day. Mrs. Constable took care of the children, which left Eleanor free to pack up the workshop, assisted by George. Edward Mason was trusted with transporting all the materials to the new location.

Joseph was impressed with the way in which everything was carefully transferred to Little Edward Street. Mrs. Constable, in her usual efficient manner, had organised the upper rooms of the house, allocating the children their bedrooms, settling Little Nell into the nursery and making the living areas comfortable and inviting.

Eleanor spent hours setting out the workrooms, giving each florist their own space in which to work. George and Edward coordinated dispatching and delivery and awaited Joseph's approval, which came very soon after they had locked away the final bolts of silk.

Eleanor was overjoyed to be in her spacious new home, which afforded her plenty of space to create new arrangements, both on paper and in the workshop. Joseph continued to add to the workforce, with some women working from home and others working alongside Eleanor in the factory.

Edward Mason worked long hours delivering materials to the women at home and then collecting their work, to be taken back to George at the factory. Once those duties were complete first thing in the morning, he set out with boxes piled high for delivery to the gentry and to hotels in fashionable parts of London.

All of the florists were working to full capacity, whether at home or in the factory, as it seemed there was a never-ending demand for floral decorations as each season came around. Eleanor ran the workshop, her meticulous attention to detail ensuring each simple spray or large arrangement received equal attention and was created to perfection.

The seasons passed—spring, summer, autumn, and finally winter, completed each year—as Eleanor and Joseph worked together to even greater success. The children were growing rapidly and the family expanded with two more births over the next few years. Abraham and Edmund Francis joined Little Nell in the nursery, until the time came for Little Nell to move into the bedroom with her sister Helen, to make room for another new baby that was coming within the next few months.

Eleanor was tired. Her pregnancy was not progressing well and she had little appetite for food. Joseph looked on in alarm as Eleanor lost weight and was, on many occasions, unable to complete her drawings or her work in the factory.

Mrs. Constable became more and more concerned as she watched her daughter lose the spirit that kept her creativity alive. With each passing month, Eleanor found it more and more difficult to keep up her busy schedule.

Joseph decided he must take action, and late one evening when the day was completed, he headed upstairs to find Eleanor asleep in the large armchair beside the fire. Kneeling quietly beside her, he took her hand in his. Her eyes fluttered open as she looked up at him.

"Joseph," she said softly, a gentle smile spreading across her pale face.

"Eleanor," Joseph whispered.

"I've been thinking. You have not been well for weeks now, perhaps a few days in the country would help. Let's get out of London and visit Abraham. The air will do you the world of good and Ann will nurse you back to health."

Eleanor's face lit up at the thought of seeing Abraham and Ann again. It was so long since they had been down to the farm. She pulled herself up and leaned heavily against the back of the chair.

"I'd love that, Joseph," said Eleanor as she took Joseph's hand in hers.

"I'll make the arrangements right away, my dear. We can take the train to High Wycombe and Abraham will send a cab to meet us."

In spite of the blustering weather and Eleanor's advancing pregnancy, it was a trip she was looking forward to. Mrs. Constable packed a small case, placing a number of items inside that she thought Eleanor might need, in readiness for their departure early the next morning.

Ann and Abraham were delighted to greet Joseph and

Eleanor. Ann fussed around, making sure Eleanor was warm and comfortable in Abraham's armchair. The brothers left the farmhouse to wander around the farm and walk the land down to the small stream that snaked across the fields, marking the boundary of Abraham's farm.

"Jane!" called Ann to her daughter-in-law, as the heavy door closed loudly behind the two men.

"Go to the dairy and fetch some fresh milk. Oh! And some cream as well, please."

Ann turned her anxious face towards Eleanor, not wanting to give away the shock she had felt as she had greeted her sister-in-law at the door. Gone was the grace and delicate beauty always associated with the lovely Eleanor. In her place, Ann saw a tired, fragile creature, barely able to cross the threshold into the warm and inviting room.

"You need fattening up, my girl," she said sternly to Eleanor, who smiled and said nothing.

"There's plenty of good food here, you know, and we'll have you feelin' better in no time."

"Isaac," called Ann, to her son, "fetch more wood and stoke the fire higher. Your aunt is cold."

Ann was at her best when she was giving orders and maintaining control, and this situation, she could see clearly, needed her earnest attention.

Eleanor's health improved over the next few days. A little colour returned to her cheeks as Ann sat with her, tempting her with morsels of carefully prepared food, encouraging her to eat whenever the opportunity arose.

Jane made tea and served cake every afternoon, as the two women sat quietly talking. Eleanor enjoyed the companiable silences, as she dozed in the big armchair, vacated for her by Abraham. Ann had confided in her husband the evening Eleanor and Joseph had arrived, telling him Eleanor must see a doctor. She waited for the moment when she felt she could suggest this to Eleanor.

"I'm well enough, Ann," insisted Eleanor. "I just need a little rest, that's all. We're so busy in the factory…" Eleanor's words trailed off and were left hanging in the air for Ann to grasp at, as she hoped to change Eleanor's mind.

"You need a doctor, Eleanor," Ann insisted, but her pleas fell on deaf ears, as Eleanor turned her head into the chair and closed her eyes.

Early each morning after their arrival, Joseph had walked out with Abraham, taking a keen interest in the new dairy herd Abraham was rearing, and spent the late afternoons driving in the cows for milking. Abraham was always one of the first farmers in the area to implement new farming methods. He had embraced crop rotation a number of years previously, which gave better use of his land. No more fields lying fallow, he told Joseph.

As the brothers were deep in conversation one afternoon on the far side of the farm, Abraham suddenly became aware of a tall, slim figure running towards them. They were standing in the lower fields when Isaac raised his arm and called out to the pair, his face red, his chest heaving, as he tried to catch his breath.

"Father!" he called. "Come quickly. Mother sent me, it's Aunt Eleanor."

Joseph began to run at full speed across the field, onto the footpath that ran up towards the house. Ann met him at the door.

"Eleanor's in labour," she said.

Joseph ran past her into the room and bounded up the stairs, calling as he went, "Eleanor! Eleanor!"

Ann hurried closely behind, following him to the bedside.

"It's too early," Joseph cried, trying to control the panic

and alarm in his voice, as he bent over Eleanor.

Joseph turned away from the bed, his face contorted with agony at the sight of his wife in such pain, and called desperately to Ann, "Call the doctor! Quickly, Ann!"

Turning again towards his wife, he knelt beside the bed, grasping hold of her hand, at the same time as he tore a white handkerchief from his pocket to wipe her brow. He noticed her shallow breathing; the beads of perspiration forming across her pale cheeks.

Outside, night was drawing in, and a strong wind rattled the windows on the other side of the room. Joseph looked up, while a terrible stab of fear and anguish plunged across his chest, as Ann entered the room.

"Isaac has gone for Dr. Goodwin, Joseph. I'll stay with Eleanor. You go downstairs and wait for the doctor to arrive," Ann instructed, as soon as she saw the distraught look that had spread across Joseph's face.

"Leave it to me, now," Ann insisted, as she moved closer to Eleanor's bedside.

One look at her dear sister-in-law told her the woman was in serious trouble as she was about to give birth. Ann sent up a silent prayer.

"Please God, no! Not Eleanor, with all those tiny children to look after."

Eleanor was barely conscious when Dr. Goodwin arrived. A stout, elderly man with a full set of whiskers, he hurried into the room, clutching a large black medical bag that he placed on the floor beside the bed.

"I'll need more towels and some hot water. Quick as you can!" Dr. Goodwin said as he tore off his jacket and plunged his hand inside of his bag.

Eleanor moaned quietly on the bed, her face ashen, her eyes closed. Dr. Goodwin worked swiftly, preparing for the birth of

Eleanor's child.

Abraham sat with Joseph downstairs in the kitchen, trying his best to console his distraught brother. Joseph was numb with fear. Isaac entered quietly. The room was heavy with silence, and despair hung in the air, as he addressed his father.

"I'll be in the milking shed, Father, if you need me. Jane is making tea."

Abraham looked up and nodded at his departing son.

The grandfather clock chimed nine times in the hallway, bringing Joseph back into the present.

"It's been over an hour now, Abe," he said to his brother.

"Be patient, Joe," Abraham said softly. "I'll fetch a little whisky for us."

No sooner had Abraham returned with two glasses of whisky, than Ann entered the room and flopped down in the vacant chair close to the doorway.

"You have a son, Joe," she smiled, as she looked into the sad face of her brother-in-law.

"And Eleanor?" Joseph asked quietly.

"The doctor will be down in a moment and he'll talk to you, but for now, Eleanor is sleeping."

Joseph's chest heaved, as he clutched the arms of the chair, lowering himself down into it.

"Thank you, my dear," Joseph said, his voice barely a whisper, as he placed his hand over his eyes.

"A little more whisky, Joe?" Abraham asked, knowing his brother was desperate for comfort.

Abraham rose to his feet, clutching the bottle in his hand and poured the amber spirit into Joseph's glass. There was a commotion in the room above and Ann flew to the stairs.

"What is it, Doctor?" she called as she mounted the stairs and flung open the bedroom door.

Dr. Goodwin's face was heavy with sadness. The sleeves

of his shirt were rolled up to his elbows, and strands of thin, grey hair hung down over his eyes. Beads of perspiration stood out on his heavily lined brow. Ann noticed his exhaustion as he leaned over Eleanor.

"I'm so sorry, my dear," he said, turning slightly to Ann, but not taking his eyes off of Eleanor's face.

Ann looked over to see Eleanor's lifeless body on the bed, covered only with a sheet. Uncomprehendingly, she looked back at Dr. Goodwin. Fighting back her tears, she buried her face in her hands.

Eleanor's baby slept soundly in the makeshift cradle that Ann had made for him from the drawer of her chest. His pink hands were tucked tightly into the blanket that surrounded the tiny body. He lay, just as Ann had left him an hour before, directly after his birth.

"The baby is small. He'll need a lot of attention," said Dr. Goodwin, as he packed instruments back into his medical bag.

"There was nothing more I could do for Eleanor. She hemorrhaged soon after the birth and I couldn't stem the bleeding."

Ann descended the stairs, following the doctor into the kitchen. Joseph rose to his feet.

"Doctor…?" he said in a whisper, as he looked in disbelief at Ann's tear-stained face.

Dr. Goodwin looked at the young man in front of him, seeing the dread and anguish that had suddenly descended upon Joseph, as Abraham moved forward to ease his brother back into the armchair.

"I'm so sorry," said Dr. Goodwin in a hushed tone.

Joseph fell back into the chair. His lovely, beloved Eleanor. How could he go on without her? She was everything to him, to her children, to her sisters, and to her mother. Life would never be the same for any of them.

"She was forty-one years old," he murmured through his tears.

Abraham gripped his brother's shoulder. "I'm here, Joe," was all he could say.

CHAPTER NINETEEN

Eleanor was laid to rest in the peaceful churchyard of St. John the Evangelist Church in Lacey Green. Joseph had chosen a prominent spot for her grave, one that sat just inside the low wooden gate and off the shingle pathway. The grey stone church, with its red brick trim, rose up behind her final resting place, giving shelter and protection in the years to come.

Joseph was preparing to return to London two days after the funeral, when Ann drew him aside.

"Joe, you have to think about the baby. What will you name him?" she asked.

Joseph looked at her, his face a mask of grief.

"I don't know, Ann … I…" he stammered, unable to complete his sentence

"Joe, I will engage a local girl who will travel back to London with you. Mrs. Constable will need help. Would you like me to do that?" asked Ann, having already identified a suitable girl and only waiting for Joseph to agree.

"Yes, yes, of course, Ann … do whatever you think is best," replied Joseph, as he departed the room and took to the stairs.

Eighteen-year-old Martha arrived at the farm promptly the following morning, to be greeted by Ann, who had already outlined her duties, making it clear to her that she must be available to stay in London for as long as she was required.

Martha was the oldest in a large family whose parents owned an adjoining farm. She was well used to looking after the younger children. Her mother had agreed that Martha could travel to London as the baby's nursemaid, knowing well that Ann's recommendation would keep her eldest daughter safe in the big city.

Martha was a very competent young woman, self-assured and mature for her age. Life on her father's farm had never been easy with so many mouths to feed, but Martha had always risen to the occasion when her mother needed her help the most. From a young age, she had taken responsibility for her younger siblings. The task of caring for this tiny baby did not daunt her in the least.

Martha addressed Joseph, asking him, "What's the baby's, name, sir?"

Joseph looked at the girl. Her fresh young face, fringed with golden curls, reminded him so much of Eleanor, who'd shown the same kindness, gentleness, in her earlier days. He stared blankly at Martha and murmured, "I … I don't know Martha; I haven't chosen a name yet…"

Martha hesitated before she replied, "Could we call him Walter, sir, after my father?"

Joseph was grateful to the girl for making the decision for him. He forced a smile.

"Yes, yes, of course, Martha."

The pair arrived back in London, with Martha fully in control of baby Walter, who slept soundly as they travelled, his father barely glancing at him, as the train rumbled into the London station.

Seventeen-year-old Helen met her father and Martha at the door, ushering them both inside, before she turned to look at her new baby brother. Martha held the baby out to Helen, whose grief-stricken face was flushed with tears.

Martha said gently, as she placed the baby into Helen's arms, "His name is Walter, Miss."

Joseph embraced his daughter silently, and then, leaving the two young women to care for his new son, he made his way upstairs to his bedroom.

Mary Weller arrived at the house on Sunday afternoon, to be met by Mrs. Constable. The shock of Eleanor's death written plainly on her face. Mary's stern features hid a generous heart. Now she took the tiny hands of Eleanor's mother in hers.

"You know, Mrs. Constable, that I will do whatever I can to help you," Mary said reassuringly, as she smiled into the face of the elderly woman, who seemed to have aged considerably since she had seen her last.

"Thank you, Mary," said Mrs. Constable. "Helen is a great help and we have a nursemaid for Walter."

Joseph left the house early in the mornings, returning late in the evening. He threw himself into his work, increasing new orders by 50%. The factory was hardly coping with the amount of work generated by an almost demented Joseph. The whole family had been plunged into mourning for a year and Mrs. Constable was barely coping. Her usual bright, efficient manner had dissipated with the unexpected news of her daughter's death at such a young age.

Overnight, Helen became mother to her younger brothers and to Little Nell. Martha was always ready to help her, and the two girls worked together to become the mainstays of the family.

Joseph John, Eleanor and Joseph's first son, stepped up to run the factory, his father absent most of the time. He had worked closely with his mother and knew how she liked things to be done. He continued to organise the workers, as his mother had taught him, supervising the making of each flower, spray, and bouquet. He gave the same amount of attention to each order as his mother had done. He was as meticulous as she had been.

Mary was a frequent visitor to the house, seeking out young Helen on every visit, to ensure she was coping with her additional responsibilities. The task was immense for such a young woman, thought Mary.

Walter thrived in the care of Martha. He was a contented and happy baby, giving his nursemaid no trouble at all, sleeping through the nights, unaware of the grief circulating throughout the house at his mother's death.

The family survived the first year after Eleanor's death, the period of mourning over by that point. Joseph began slowly to live again in a world without his beloved Eleanor. He was grateful to his older children, Helen and Joseph John, for the way in which they had relieved him of the burdens he carried.

Joseph John was still young, he reminded himself, but the boy had always shown a degree of responsibility far above his age. His serious nature and quiet demeanor gave only a glimpse of the hidden strength that lay beneath the surface and Joseph knew his son was dependable and hard-working.

In spite of the fact that both Helen and Joseph John had stepped in to do an amazing job, Helen with the children and Joseph John in the factory, Joseph knew the family was falling apart, slowly and quietly, as the aftermath of Eleanor's death had left them rudderless.

Eleanor had always been the driving force behind Joseph's ambition. She stood with him shoulder to shoulder in their endeavours to create a successful business. She had been an equal partner, and Joseph knew he could not have achieved the like without Eleanor's wise guidance.

She, after all, had been the artist, the creator of blooms,

from spring flowers to Christmas roses. Her talent had built the business overtime, out-running all competition from other flower makers in the area. How to continue in her memory was the thought that haunted Joseph during those sleepless nights, that gave no relief from the pangs of his continuing loneliness.

It was no longer enough for him to work eighteen hours a day to stem the constant flow of grief that hit him throughout the days and nights. The family were barely getting through each day. Mrs. Constable, a shadow of her former self, no longer able to run an efficient household. Instead, she retreated to her sitting room for hours on end. Helen and Martha, in her absence, kept the children washed and fed, seeing them off to school, but Joseph knew that was not enough. The family had lost its heart and he didn't know what to do about it. He couldn't think, his mind cutting off the reality of each day, so as to make it possible for him to carry on.

When Solomon and Fanny came to visit, Joseph received them on the lower floor of the house, guiding them towards his office, which overlooked the narrow street outside. Eleanor's drawings remained strewn across the table, together with her painting materials, as though she had only just left the room.

Joseph greeted them warmly.

"I'm so pleased to see you both, you know" he said, indicating that Solomon should sit in one of the large leather chairs on the opposite side of the room.

Fanny smiled warmly at her brother-in-law, and said, "Joe, I would like to go upstairs to see Mrs. Constable, if you don't mind."

"Of course, Fanny, I know she will be pleased to see you. She sees so few people these days," Joseph said.

Fanny left the room, anxious to meet Martha and to see baby Walter. Helen, she knew, was looking forward to seeing her also. Fanny understood the girl's quiet grief and wanted to make sure she was coping with all of the responsibilities that had been forced upon her since her mother's death.

Joseph took his place in the armchair next to his brother, pleased to have the comfort that Solomon always brought to him. Their business ventures had been shared in the early days and their success in business had been attributed to their mutual love of ambition and achievement.

Joseph was at a loss for the first time in his life. He had never experienced the hopelessness he felt; for his grieving, there was no relief. Eleanor had been everything to him. She was the heart of his family and the mainstay of his business. Since her death, he had sleepwalked through life, wearing his devastation for all to see.

Solomon looked across at his brother, seeing that same hopelessness etched in every new line of his face.

"How are you, Joe?" Solomon ventured, unsure of how his brother would deal with such an intrusive question.

"The light's gone from my life, Sol," said Joseph. The children need me, but I cannot rise above Eleanor's death to meet their needs." Joseph's upturned palms said it all, as his shoulders slouched and he sank deeper into the leather of the armchair.

Solomon thought deeply, before he said, "Joe, you need someone to look after you and to care for the children. Helen and Martha are doing a good job, but they are young and it's too much responsibility for both of them. Mrs. Constable has aged and will never recover from Eleanor's death."

Joseph stared into space and said, "Yes, I suppose you're right, Sol, but … I just don't know what to do anymore."

Solomon took a deep breath and hesitated before he spoke again.

"Ask Mary Weller to marry you!" he said, his voice barely audible.

Joseph's head shot up, a look of total surprise on his face. "What?!" he said.

Solomon was ready for Joseph's reaction. He thought again before uttering, "You cannot go on like this, Joe. There's too much at stake." He continued carefully, "Eleanor is relying on you to care for her children and to keep the business running. She worked so hard for your success and you cannot let her down now, Joe. You have to find a way to go on."

Joseph stretched his legs out in front of him. The very idea of marrying Mary was ridiculous, he thought. She had been a dear friend to Eleanor, it was true the children loved her, for they had known her all their lives, but … marry her?

Confusion spread across Joseph's face, as he turned to face his brother.

"The idea is outrageous!" he said sharply.

Solomon nodded, looking directly at Joseph, and asked, "Is it? Who better than Mary?" "Think about Helen, Joe. She's young, and she cannot devote her life to her younger siblings. It's not fair to ask that of her."

Is that what Eleanor would want of him? To marry Mary? he wondered. It was true that Eleanor and Mary had been very close friends and he knew that Mary loved each one of Eleanor's children as though they were her own. Mrs. Constable was aging fast. What of her? The thought struck him. Eleanor's mother had given so much to him and the family. She was another dependent whose life relied upon him.

Suddenly, Joseph was overcome with emotion at the thought of the huge demands that were being asked of him, and he knew, in that moment, that he could not meet them alone. Solomon spoke again, interrupting his thoughts.

"You have eight children, Joe! Walter is barely a year old. How long d'you think you can go on like this?" urged Solomon.

"My god, Sol!" said Joseph. "That's asking a hell of a lot from Mary."

"She can take it, Joe. Mary's one strong woman!" Solomon said with certainty.

Joseph fell into a silence that Solomon did not want to interrupt, knowing his brother needed to think about the idea he had put to him.

Solomon rose from his chair and put a brotherly arm around Joseph's shoulders.

"Think about it, Joe." Solomon's voice was gentle and encouraging. "As I said, you can't do this alone."

Solomon left Joseph staring out of the window and climbed the stairs to find his wife.

CHAPTER TWENTY

Joseph and Mary were married quietly three months later. The children were overjoyed that Mary would be living with them and did everything they could to make her feel welcome in her new home. It was a huge relief to Helen, who would, of course, continue to care for her younger siblings, but the weight had been lifted from her shoulders.

It was decided that Martha would stay with the family, much to Helen's delight. The two girls had become great friends and Martha was more than willing to stay on in London. Mary encouraged the girls to take daily walks, to get out of the house for a short while each day, since she was there to care for Walter.

Mary talked to Helen and Martha, telling them their duties would be shared from then on. Mrs. Constable was also in need of daily assistance, she said, and the girls agreed to help Mary with her care. Mary noticed immediately after she had married and moved into Little Edward Street, that Mrs. Constable was far from the woman she used to be. The older woman's mind wandered when Mary sat with her in the afternoons.

With Mary in the house, Joseph slowly began to return to life; she saw fleeting glimpses of the old Joseph, but she knew it would take time for him to recover, even partially, from Eleanor's death. He no longer worried about his children or about Mrs. Constable, knowing that he could rely on Mary to take care of everything. Meanwhile, he continued to throw himself into running his expanding business, leaving the house each morning as soon as he had checked that everything was working well in the factory and the dispatching areas.

By late summer, Joseph could smile again and agreed to walk in Regent's Park with Mary, taking with them Edmund Francis, Little Nell, and Walter. Joseph strolled beside his wife, watching his young children skipping and playing as they chased each other between the ancient oaks that were already beginning to lose their leaves.

For the first time since Eleanor's death, Joseph felt the warmth of life return within him. He stole a sideways glance at his wife, noticing how a gentle smile lit her face.

"I owe everything to you, Mary," said Joseph softly as they walked. "I will never be able to repay you for what you have given us all."

Mary turned her head and smiled. "'Tis you, Joseph, who have given me everything. Your love, your respect, and your children. I owe you much."

Joseph was taken by surprise at Mary's words. "Are you happy?" he asked tentatively.

"I am very happy, Joseph. Thank you," she said.

Martha had laid tea for them when they returned home and swiftly took charge of the three young children, whisking them off to their beds. Over the next couple of years, Joseph John took on more responsibility, working diligently at his father's instructions, eager to learn and to relieve his father of the stress he knew he carried.

Joseph John begged his father to slow down, as he explained the factory was working at maximum capacity. The staff in every department were overloaded with work, making it obvious to Joseph John that he would have to come up with a plan to cope with the extra business Joseph hadbrought in since his mother's death.

Joseph reluctantly saw the sense in his son's reasoning and began taking more time off from the business. He took Mary down to the farm to meet Abraham and Ann and to St. John's Wood to visit Solomon and Fanny.

As Joseph walked from his office onto the factory floor one day, he noticed Joseph John talking to a fair-haired young woman. She was tall and slim, neat in her appearance, with a quick smile that spread easily across her pale face.

Joseph noticed the couple appeared to be in deep conversation, as they bent over a large arrangement of pale pink roses. The young woman held a bunch of crimson carnations in her hands, her long fingers encircling the stems. Joseph John was instructing her, he could see, his son's hands pointing to the shape of the arrangement sitting on the table in front of them. The woman nodded in agreement from time to time as Joseph John spoke to her.

There was something about the stance of the couple that interested Joseph and he took the next opportunity to speak to his son about it. Joseph had not seen the young woman in the workroom before and he mentioned this to his son.

"Louisa is new here, Father," explained Joseph John. "She has moved from Brighton with her family."

Joseph nodded, "I see," was all he said.

In the months that followed, Joseph became increasingly aware of his son's interest in the young Louisa. He noticed Louisa's work table had been moved closer to the corner where his son worked. The two were often seen chatting in the stores area. He heard the brief discussions over colours andfabrics as he passed by on the way into his own office.

Joseph John approached the table where his sister worked in the far corner of the workshop. Helenkept herself apart from the chatter and noise of the factory, preferring to work alone. Helen's darkcurls were tied at the nape of her neck with blue ribbon, but long, silky strands had escaped the bow, to fall over her eyes.

Helen had inherited her mother's artistic ability. As a small child, she had spent long hours sitting at Eleanor's elbow, watching her mother's long, slender fingers create flowers, both in bud and full bloom, using pastel colours from her palette. Helen shared Eleanor's love of art, but her style was strikingly different from that of her mother.

~

"Helen!' Joseph John called out, as he came towards her.

Helen looked up, to see her brother striding with purpose. There was an urgency in his step and Helen wondered what was coming:

"I want to compliment you, Helen, on your work. Father is delighted," he said as he smiled downat Helen's serious face, while she looked up at him.

"Oh?" she said.

"You know…" Joseph John continued, "your ideas are so very different from mother's, but equally beautiful."

Helen was surprised to receive such a compliment from her brother. Neither he, nor her father, had commented on her work before.

"Mother used pastel shades … her work was delicate, having a fragile beauty all of its own, but you…" Joseph John's voice trailed away, as he peered thoughtfully at the painting in front of him.

"Yes?" said Helen.

"Well, I was just thinking," replied Joseph John. "Your colours are bold, vibrant, echoing the new,modern style. You are braver than mother!" he laughed.

"Yes, I am," Helen smiled.

"It's time to move on Helen, to a new era. Father is tired and wants to spend more time with Mary. I am to take over the business. I discussed it with Father a few days ago."

Joseph had not intended to confide in Helen just yet, but the thought struck him, as he looked over her work, that they were the new generation, and it was they who would take the business into the future.

Joseph John had been aware for a long time that it would be his responsibility to ensure the success of the company, as many lives depended upon it. He had assured his father, as he looked directly into his eyes, that he had the ability to sail the ship through the choppy waters of the future.

"I'm with you, John," Helen said. "Together we'll go forward and carry on the legacy Mother created from those scraps of fabric, lying on the floor in grandfather's tailoring shop!" Her tinkling laughter brought joy to Joseph John's heart.

It came as no surprise to Joseph when his son asked to speak to him privately early one morning, before the busy day began. Joseph was walking through the factory making his last-minute checks before setting out for appointments on Oxford Street and The Strand.

Joseph John followed his father into the office and closed the door behind him. He stood anxiously in front of his father's desk, waiting for Joseph to seat himself. When his father looked up, he began, "I have wanted to speak to you for some time, Father" Joseph John said hesitantly, his voice husky with nerves, as he looked at his father.

"Yes?" Joseph was not going to make this easy for his son. He knew what was coming and was in full agreement, but he waited to hear what the boy had to say.

"It's like this, Father" Joseph John started. "I'd like to ask Louisa to marry me." A sigh of relief escaped his lips, as he waited for his father to comment.

Joseph said nothing, leaving the young man standing in front of him full of apprehension. At last, he spoke. "I have yet to meet Louisa, John," said Joseph. Joseph John knew that when his father used the familiar name to distinguish himself from his father, there would be no objections. He began to breathe a little easier, and his shoulders relaxed, as he asked, "May I bring Louisa to tea on Sunday, Father?"

There was no hint of a smile on Joseph's face, but he nodded and spoke. "I will ask Mary."

With that, Joseph rose from his desk and wished his son good morning.

CHAPTER TWENTY-ONE

Joseph John and Louisa were married in late spring of the following year. The ceremony took place in the parish church of St. Martin-in-the-Fields, sited in the northeast corner of Trafalgar Square.

Joseph looked on as his son took his vows, offering the young woman beside him comfort and love in their life together. It was times like this when Joseph thought of Eleanor, sad that she was not at his side, but grateful for the love of Mary, who never failed him.

A new office was built in the corner of the factory, close to the office occupied by Joseph. Joseph John was pleased to have a quiet space of his own, where he could stack the accounting ledgers, along with the designs that Helen frequently brought to him.

Louisa's table was moved into a more prominent position in the factory, where she could see all of the florists at work. Her keen eye took note of every arrangement that was being worked on. She did not follow the easy-going style of her brother, who managed in a friendly, informal manner. Louisa made few friends; her stern countenance did not invite idle chatter or gossip. She increased production by glaring meaningfully at any florist who turned her head to engage her neighbour in a comment.

Louisa did not possess the gentle manner of her husband, whose kindly encouragement brought smiles to the faces of his employees. Instead, Louisa maintained strict adherence to the rules she set as soon as she took over supervision of the factory, immediately after her marriage.

Joseph John admired his wife's ability to manage well. But it had to be said, he was often somewhat disturbed at the lack of empathy Louisa had for the staff. This aspect of her character concerned him, but there was no doubt she was good for business, which gave him the opportunity to concentrate on other matters at hand.

Joseph had taught his son the accounting procedures and Joseph John's beautiful handwriting kept careful records in the heavy leather-bound ledgers that his father checked every month. Joseph John ordered the fabric and took stock frequently of what materials had been used, transcribing the number of bales ordered into another set of ledgers.

Joseph kept a keen eye on everything, satisfying himself that his son and daughter-in-law were very capable of running the business. He was extremely pleased with the new measures introduced by Joseph John, ensuring that orders were processed and sent for delivery as soon as possible after they were received.

Mary ran the household with Martha's help. Helen was relieved of her duties, as she spent more and more time downstairs in the factory.

Mary noticed that Mrs. Constable had not been well for a while. It was difficult persuading the old lady to eat; her mind was wandering more than ever and she hardly came out of her bedroom. Mary thought perhaps this was due to the fact she had such difficulty walking and moving around.

If Mrs. Constable refused to leave her bedroom, Mary took tea into her and sat beside her bed in the afternoons. On most occasions, she read to her, but seeing the vacant look in her eyes, Mary would often tiptoe from the room, as Mrs. Constable dozed off.

On one such afternoon, as summer turned into autumn, Mary passed by the open door of Mrs. Constable's sitting room, noticing the curtains had been pulled across the window, shutting out the light, making the room dark in the early afternoon. As Mary always went in to see Mrs. Constable first thing in the morning to draw the curtains in her bedroom and her sitting room, she had a feeling of unease and stepped through the door, calling out to Mrs. Constable as she entered the room. Mary's calls were met with an eerie silence and as soon as she entered the bedroom, she understood why.

Slumped on the floor beside the bed was the unmoving figure of Mrs. Constable in her nightgown, her unseeing eyes wide open, looking upward to the ceiling. Mary rushed to her side, but realised it was too late. The old lady had fallen as she tried to get back into the bed.

The doctor arrived an hour later to pronounce Mrs. Constable dead, just as Joseph walked through the door downstairs. When Mary called out to him, he ran up the stairs to see the doctor bending over his mother-in-law.

"What happened, Mary?" asked Joseph.

"She's gone, Joe," said Mary in a hushed tone, as she stood at his elbow.

The doctor snapped his bag closed, as he said, "I will send for the coroner."

Joseph nodded at the doctor and held out his hand to him, as he said, "Thank you, Doctor."

Mrs. Constable had been a huge support to him when Eleanor died. He could not have managed the children and the household without her, but she was gone, and he grieved the loss of the woman who had given them all so much. Mary saw the sadness Mrs. Constable's death brought to her husband; she was his link to the past and to Eleanor, she knew, but she said nothing.

The death of Mrs. Constable plunged the family into mourning once again, but business had to go on. Joseph John, Louisa, and Helen were at the helm, although Joseph was still out selling in the West End, bringing home each day, a bag bulging with orders to be filled.

Louisa kept her firm grip on the workshop, where evermore floral arrangements were dispatched each day to large hotels in various parts of London. There was never an occasion when shoddy work slipped by her beady eye. She inspected every flower and petal in each arrangement, sending back work that she considered to be less than perfect. Production became a lot more efficient, but it changed the atmosphere in the workshop, which did not go unnoticed by Joseph.

Autumn slipped away, as winter swept in with howling gales and torrents of rain that slashed against the window panes at night, frightening the children. Mary ran from room to room, comforting the little ones, but the nights were long and the days were cold. Joseph stoked the fires, finding it difficult to keep the house warm.

Nine-year old Edmund Francis was restless and unwell. Mary sat with him, trying to coax him to drink some warm milk, but the child pushed the cup away, turning his red, flushed face to the wall. Mary took him from beneath the blankets and held him close to her, as he whimpered into her breast. She rocked him back and forth, trying to soothe his restless body, but he twisted and turned in her arms, attempting to throw off the blanket that Mary had wrapped around him.

Mary took a cool cloth to wipe Edmund's brow and was alarmed at the heat coming from his tiny body. She called Joseph, who hurried into the room to see his son fighting for breath. He knew immediately that the situation was dire. Turning to Mary, Joseph said, "I'm going to get the doctor, Mary. Keep him as cool as you can."

On hearing the urgency in her father's voice, Helen appeared in the doorway, with Martha standing closely behind her.

"Mary, what is it?" cried Helen.

"Edmund is burning up. We have to keep him as cool as we can. Please get me some cold water in a bowl and some more cloths." Mary's calm exterior belied the fear she felt within her, as she continued to rock Edmund back and forth, talking quietly to him.

The doctor arrived fifteen minutes later with Joseph close on his heels. Helen and Martha left the room as the doctor took Edmund Francis from Mary's outstretched arms. The child was still, as the doctor began to remove his clothes, peering closely at the red blotches spreading across the boy's pale chest, which rose and fell as Edmund gasped for breath.

"The child has measles," the doctor said, looking directly at Joseph. "He must be isolated immediately. Nobody is to enter this room, other than you, Mary." The doctor's gaze shifted to Mary, who nodded.

"Yes, Doctor," she said quietly.

"Food is to be left at the door and all plates and cutlery are to be sterilised in boiling water." As an afterthought, the doctor added, "Oh, and keep everything you use for Edmund Francis away from the other children. We can't risk further infections."

The doctor's face was grave, as he shook hands with Joseph and nodded to Mary as he left the room.

For the next three days, Mary remained in the bedroom with Edmund, administering to his every need. Although the child refused to eat, Mary was able to spoon feed him with Martha's broth. He would sip a little water from a teaspoon, but Mary could see there was little improvement in his condition.

Mary stood at the window, looking out across the rooftops of buildings lying behind their own property. Grey slate stretched out to meet a blackening horizon, as yet more rain swept in to batter the red brick that stood unyielding against the onslaught. Forked lightning flashed across the sky, illuminating the dark room. A crash of thunder, directly overhead, brought a cry from the bed in the far corner of the room. Mary turned abruptly to see a struggling Edmund Francis, his frail body thrashing about on top of the covers he had thrown off in a desperate attempt to cool his burning body.

Mary gathered the little boy up in her arms, whispering softly into his ear, until he became calmer, his breath coming a little easier as he relaxed in her arms. Mary rocked him until he fell asleep, when she carried him over to the armchair beneath the window and sank into the softness of the old, familiar padding that gave her warmth and comfort. She was so tired and desperate with worry for Edmund, whom she loved as dearly as though he was her own. She had watched over him since Eleanor's death, as she had done for all of the children. Baby Walter, who had never known his mother, clung to Martha, who carried him around on her hip for most of the day. These children were so precious to her, she thought, as she fell asleep, with her head resting against the wing of the chair.

Dawn broke, and a stream of light filtered through the window, flooding the room with unexpected winter sunshine. Mary woke with a start, instinctively tightening her hold on Edmund Francis, whose unmoving body did not respond.

Her cries brough Helen running into the room. Mary held Edmund up to her face, embracing his inert body.

"Fetch your father," is all she could say at that moment.

Helen fled from the room, calling out for her father, who emerged from his bedroom to stumble through the hallway.

"Mary! Mary! What is it? I'm coming!"

By the time Joseph entered the sick room, Mary had risen from the chair and had placed the body of Edmund back into the bed and had drawn the sheet up to cover his face.

"Oh, Joe!" she cried, as she threw herself into his arms. Joseph peered over her shoulder at the lifeless body of his son, a dreadful realisation creeping over him. With his arm still around his wife, he moved to kneel beside the bed, taking Edmund's hand in his own. This man, who had known such sadness in his life, wept as he cradled his son, holding him tight to his chest, mouthing soft words, as he brushed his lips across Edmund's face.

"My beautiful boy…" he cried. "My beautiful boy."

Rising from the bedside, he turned to Mary, whose face was white and pinched with shock, silent tears running down her cheeks. Joseph held her tight.

"There was nothing more you could have done for him, Mary," he said gently, as Mary sobbed into his shoulder.

The doctor arrived as early workers filed into the factory below, taking their seats in silence. When news reached Louisa, she went immediately in search of Mary, whom she found sitting at the scrubbed topped table in the kitchen, her head buried in her hands. Dark strands of hair covered her eyes, which Louisa saw were red with crying.

"You've been wonderful, Mary," said Louisa, as she knelt down beside her. "Now you need some rest, so come on, I'll bring tea to your room."

Mary rose slowly to walk back down the hallway to her bedroom, where Joseph sat motionless on the side of the bed, his face etched with pain and sorrow. He looked up as Mary entered the room and gestured her to sit beside him.

Placing his arm across her shoulders, he looked into her tired eyes, to see his own suffering reflected there. It was a moment before he spoke.

"Mary," his voice was barely a whisper. "I want to go home"

Joseph stared ahead of him, seeing nothing but the blackness that grew before his eyes, the unbearable grief that engulfed him. Turning once again to Mary, he bent his head and spoke.

"Let us go to Abraham. I can't stay here."

Mary nodded. "As soon as we have buried Edmund Francis, we will go to stay with Abraham."

Joseph patted her hand. "Thank you, my dear. Now you must rest. I'll make all the arrangements."

Joseph moved towards the door and Mary heard his footsteps on the stairs as he descended into the factory, calling out for Joseph John as he went.

"John! Bring me the latest entries in the ledgers, if you will."

CHAPTER TWENTY-TWO

Joseph stole a glance at Mary, sleeping soundly beside him, as he turned to rise from the warmth of the bed. Dawn was barely breaking; a shaft of grey light forced its way into the darkened room.

Mary did not stir as Joseph moved silently around the room, looking for the clothes he had so carelessly discarded the night before. The journey down to the country from London, the previous day had been a long and tiring one and both Joseph and Mary had taken to their beds in the early evening, accompanied by cups of warm milk.

Joseph glanced out of the window as he passed on his way to the door, to see the hunched figure of Isaac in the yard below, bracing himself against the onslaught of a heavy wind, as he was making his way towards the milking shed.

The sleeping household did not hear Joseph's soft tread, as he found his way downstairs into the hallway to put on a heavy wool overcoat and to pull on his boots. He lifted the latch and walked out into the farmyard to the welcome call of a cockerel, who strutted up and down inside the wire compound, his red-crested head thrown back, calling all farm hands to work.

Billy was driving the last of the cows into the milking shed, as Joseph turned the corner.

Billy lifted his arm to wave and called out, "Mornin' to

you, sir."

Joseph nodded and replied, "A good morning to you too, Billy."

Billy was fourteen years old, the eldest son of Abraham's closest neighbour and already a great help to Isaac, who had taken over the complete running of the farm. Abraham, well into his eighties, spent most of his time sitting in the old armchair beside the blackened range, carefully waited upon by his devoted wife, Ann.

Isaac looked up as Joseph entered the shed.

"Mornin', Uncle," he called from beneath a large black and white cow, who stood patiently waiting to be milked.

"Good morning, Isaac," Joseph said as he approached his nephew's side.

"This is a fine-looking herd you have," said Joseph, as he admired the stock.

"'Tis, Uncle" Isaac smiled. "Thanks to Pa, who always bought high quality beasts and from then on, we've reared our own." Joseph noted the pride in Isaac's words. He smiled and nodded, as Isaac explained, "We have one of the best dairy herds around these parts, with continued demand for our milk and cream."

Joseph walked between the rows of cows, patting each one on its boney rump. As he neared the open doors, he turned to call over his shoulder to Isaac.

"You're a good son, Isaac," he said. "Just like my own John. See you at breakfast!"

With that, he left the barn to walk briskly along the muddy footpath leading down to the stream that meandered along the boundary of the farm and into a small spinney. Tall black limbs protruded upwards into a dark sky, as frost crunched beneath his boots. Joseph's breath came in short bursts, the cold, damp air filling his lungs.

Moving deeper into the belt of trees, Joseph came upon an upturned log and sank down mercifully onto the moss-covered wood. Large rooks flew above, as he lowered his head into his hands and wept. He wept for Eleanor. Beautiful, talented Eleanor, whom he continued to miss more each day, and for their small son, Edmund Francis, born out of their love for each other. He wept for the despair he felt, in spite of the love that Mary gave so freely to him and the children.

Joseph knew he had to find a way forward. Soon it would be spring and these very same trees would come alive with new buds. Birds would be busy building nests, and the cycle of nature would begin all over again. His thoughts of the coming spring lifted him up and out of his desperate grief. He imagined the warmth of the sun on his back, during those long summer days to come. Oh! How he longed to see new blossoms on the trees and to feel the wet dew beneath his feet, to watch the meadows come alive with early primroses, and later, in June, to walk the bluebell woods, with a collie dog at his heels.

New hope flooded his body, as he pictured the scene, filling his senses with purpose.

"I'm coming home, Pa," he cried out aloud, to his long-dead father. "I'm coming home."

By the time Joseph returned to the farmhouse, Mary was in the kitchen with Ann. The delicious aroma of eggs and sizzling bacon, together with freshly baked bread, rose to meet him, as he pulled off his muddy boots.

"There you are, Joe," Mary called out to him. "Just in time for breakfast."

Ann hurried forward with a steaming mug of tea.

"Here, drink this, Joe. You must be frozen," she said.

Mary looked up from the table, where she was placing a large basket of fresh rolls and butter, surprised to see her husband's face aglow with happiness. She stared at him, not knowing what to make of his ruddy cheeks and open smile, something she had not seen in months—indeed, well before the death of Edmund.

Isaac joined the family for breakfast as Jane returned from feeding the chickens and Abraham rose from his chair to join the family at the table, which was laden with the best food the farm had to offer. Joseph looked around at his family, listening to the different conversations that were carried on between them all. He ate ravenously, enjoying every mouthful of the freshly-laid eggs and home-cured bacon, leaving behind him the last few days of deep and bitter unhappiness.

After breakfast, Abraham whistled to the sleeping dog, who rose immediately to stand at his master's heels, his tail wagging back and forth.

"You comin', Joe?" Abraham asked. "I like to walk the farm first thing every mornin'. You know, check the fences, take a look at the stock. Jane and Ann will take care of the dairy and the chickens."

With that, the two brothers left the house, warmly clad in heavy overcoats and sturdy rubber boots. They walked in silence for a good five minutes before Abraham ventured to speak.

"You're looking better this mornin', Joe" he said. "The country air's doin' you good." He smiled as he looked at Joseph.

Joseph did not reply immediately, but gathered his thoughts. Both men walked on in silence, Abraham giving his brother the time he needed to assemble the ideas that were forming in his head. He could see the struggle within, the turmoil that was churning over and over as his brother walked into the wind.

Joseph spoke after a short while. "I miss the countryside, Abe," he said. "I'll always be a farmer."

Abraham was surprised to hear his brother speak such words and said to him, "You've a good life in London, though, Joe."

Joseph nodded and said, "I do, Abe, but John and Louisa are more than capable of running the business now. They have plenty of help."

Abraham stopped in his tracks and turned to face Joseph "What are you sayin', Joe?" he asked.

The final conclusion had come to Joseph. He spun around to look directly at his brother, his mind firm and excited at the prospects he was about to outline to Abraham.

"I'm leaving London, Abe. There are just too many memories there," explained Joseph. "I'm going to buy a farm here in Oxfordshire."

Abraham was stunned. Placing his arm on his brother's shoulder, he asked, "Are you sure that's what you want to do, to leave it all behind?"

Joseph smiled broadly. "I've never been a city boy, you know, Abe. In spite of everything, I've always longed for the country, but Eleanor was born and bred in London and it was where she belonged, but now things are different and I know Mary will be with me in this."

Abraham grabbed Joseph's hand and shook it firmly. "In that case, Joe, we'll go to the agent first thing tomorrow. Let's see what he has to offer in the way of farms for sale!" Abraham laughed out loud, a deep chuckle that spun its way through the naked limbs of the poplar trees that crowded together in the thicket.

When Joseph returned to the house, Mary was sitting alone in the kitchen. Jane was in the dairy, serving a long queue of villagers wanting fresh milk. Ann was cooing to her chickens as she collected the eggs from the nesting boxes, carefully placing them in a large bowl to be taken into the farm house where they would be washed and packed, ready for sale.

Joseph pulled up an armchair close to the range, and stretching out his long legs, he looked directly at Mary.

"Mary?" he asked. "Will you come home with me to Oxfordshire, to a farm of our own?"

Mary smiled. Her fair hair, flecked with grey, was tied carefully back and held in place with a black ribbon. Mary had aged over the past few weeks, her tired face deeply lined with anxiety. Before she could answer, Joseph broke into her thoughts, saying, "We'll bring all the children with us; the older boys can help around the farm and Martha will assist you with the younger children. Walter is devoted to her."

Mary's eyes welled with tears. "Oh, Joe," she cried. "I would love that. I've lived in London all my life, but it's time for a change."

Joseph felt triumphant. "I knew you'd agree, Mary," he said. "Abe is taking me in the morning to meet the agent, to see what he has for sale in this area."

As Joseph spoke the words, he recognised a new chapter in his life opening up before him, a time when his children would run through the fields, as he himself had done in earlier days. He would teach the boys to fish; he would acquaint them with the names of birds that flew overhead. They would know a life of freedom and fresh air, something that no amount of money could buy.

"I'm a sheep man myself, Mary," Joseph explained. "Abe has always liked cows, but me? I like sheep and baby lambs in springtime."

Mary moved closer to Joseph. "I will be very happy in the countryside with you, Joe" she said. "The children will benefit from the country air and from the best fresh food."

Joseph was quiet once again, deep in thought. "It's best we let John and Louisa have Little Edward Street. After all, they have a growing family and they will need more space as time goes on. They will live over the shop, as we've done. The business is in very capable hands. There's no need to worry, Mary."

~

A few days after visiting the agent, Joseph and Mary returned to London to break the news to the children and to ask Martha if she would move with them to Oxfordshire. The children were excited as Joseph told them of his childhood spent in the country with his father. Times had undoubtedly been hard, with little money to feed the large family, but days spent working alongside Henry had left an indelible mark, and he wanted the same memories for his children.

Martha greeted the news with excitement, when Mary told her of Joseph's plan to return home to Oxfordshire. She knew her own family would be overjoyed to have her close to them again.

Joseph John saw the change in his father as soon as he arrived home. Gone was the gaunt and haunted look that had taken hold of his father since the death of Edmund Francis, to be replaced by a sprightly step and a gleam in his eyes. When Joseph outlined his plans for the farm to Joseph John, as they sat together in Joseph's office early one morning, Joseph John clapped his father on the back.

"That's wonderful news, Father. I will take care of everything here in the factory."

Joseph looked at his son fondly. "I know you will, son," was all he said.

With spring just around the corner, it was only a matter of a few weeks before Joseph became the proud owner of a fifty-acre farm on the outskirts of Aston Rowant, a small village nestled beneath the northwest escarpment of the Chiltern Hills. The area was alive with colourful butterflies that fluttered silently around the heads of wild spring flowers. Red kites flew overhead, bringing a squeal from one of the children as soon as they were spotted. Tiny orchids grew in sheltered spots, away from feet that could trample their delicate heads. Beech, yew, and juniper trees gave shelter to wildlife, as small animals scampered from the safety of their hideouts into the open fields.

The low rambling farmhouse provided plenty of room for the children. A large kitchen garden was fenced off from the farmyard and was already newly planted with spring vegetables. The barns were in need of repair, but there was plenty of local labour to take care of that. A spring-fed pond sat in the far corner of the property, surrounded by rushes and thick hawthorn. As Joseph walked the acreage, he noted that all the fences and gates were in good order, with a few minor repairs to be carried out later on in the season. There was no urgency for that at the moment, he told himself.

When Joseph returned to the house, the younger children were climbing over a disused cart in the orchard, their laughter echoing around the farm. Martha sat perched on a log, with Walter clinging to her skirts. As she gently placed him down on the ground, he whimpered, unsure of his new surroundings, so that Martha had to lift him back into her lap, where he sat contentedly watching, as the older children jumped and squealed, running between the old, gnarled fruit trees.

Joseph was surprised at how quickly his children took to life in the country. After all, they had been born and brought up in London, with only the occasional visits to Abraham's farm. Charles, in particular, took to farming immediately, as his father Joseph taught him everything he could remember from the days he walked beside his father.

When Abraham and Joseph went off to market to look at sheep, it was Charles who asked if he might go with them. He had taken a keen interest in sheep and had made it his business to learn about different breeds, surprising his father with his knowledge when he discussed the breeds they might buy at market.

Helen had remained behind in London. Her love of art and flower making made her an important part of the business. Joseph John had wanted her to stay, as he relied heavily on her for new designs.

Joseph John had taken over from his father and was out selling while Louisa managed most of the flower production. Under Joseph John's careful guidance, the business flourished, providing income for Joseph to set up the newly acquired farm.

With Charles by his side, Joseph walked the boundary of his farm each morning, pointing out to Charles the changing landscape as spring came and went. Every tree and bush was in full bloom as summer crept in.

With each day, Joseph's broken heart became whole once again. The companionship of his son Charles, coupled with the knowledge that his oldest son Joseph John was in London taking care of the business he and Eleanor had worked so hard to build, gave him strength.

Mary was happy; she loved the younger children and they loved her, remembering little of their own mother. Her days were filled with domestic duties, which brought her the greatest of pleasures.

Ann had given Mary some chickens and a cockerel, that she might start her own flock, in order to provide meat and eggs for the family. Little Nell was Mary's shadow and walked with her every morning to feed the chickens and collect the eggs. She took charge of the day-old chicks, their yellow, fluffy bodies resting gently in her palms as she soothed them, making cooing noises as Mary filled the hoppers with seed.

When night fell and darkness covered the land, Joseph took

himself off to a quiet place, falling to his knees to give thanks for his bountiful land and for the guidance that had brought him to such a cherished spot. At last, he could begin to live again with all of the pleasures life had to offer.

CHAPTER TWENTY-THREE

Life at Warren Farm for Joseph and his family was idyllic. Charles was eager to learn everything he could and spent hours out in the pasture with the sheep. He built pens and enclosures to house newly orphaned lambs and any ewes that were injured while grazing in the fields. Charles and Joseph walked the land early each morning, checking on fencing, water barrels, and troughs, ensuring there was a good supply of fresh, clean water for the animals.

When a new litter of puppies was born at Abraham's farm, Ann wrapped two black and white collie pups in an old blanket and set off with her basket for Warren Farm. Little Nell claimed the puppy with a large black patch over its left eye and Charles took ownership of the other one, naming her Bonny.

Little Nell's dog, Patch, never left her side. He trotted at her heels each morning when she went to the hen house and waited patiently outside the wire fencing as she tended the hens and collected the eggs.

Charles was busy training his sheepdog to answer to his whistle. Bonny's quick and sharp mind soon made her the perfect companion. She was fast and alert, as she snapped at the heels of any wayward sheep that thought about straying from the round-up. Joseph was impressed when he watched his son give orders to Bonny and was delighted at the way Charles had taken to country life.

Early in November, before the first frosts arrived, communication came from Jonathan in Australia. Joseph was always pleased to hear from his brother, but Jonathan's letters came only sporadically over the years and took many months to arrive by steam ship.

Joseph took the letter into the house and, pulling up his chair, close to the blackened range, he took a knife to open the bulky package. Jonathan's neat handwriting in black ink ran across the page, his letters formed carefully with the precision that Jonathan applied to everything he did.

Joseph read quickly, anxious for the latest news from Australia, but his mind could not believe what his eyes were telling him. Jonathan and Jane were coming home! Jonathan wrote that he had three large farms, which he was going to leave in the care of his two sons. He had sufficient money to retire comfortably in England, he said.

It would be spring of the following year before Jonathan and Jane arrived in England, but Joseph was already preparing for the arrival of his brother and sister-in-law. There was little time to get a letter back to Jonathan before the departure date, but plans were already afoot to accommodate the new arrivals.

Mary watched the joy rise in her husband at the thought of seeing his brother again after so many years. He talked to her of the times he and his brothers worked alongside their father in the fields. He talked of their hunting for rabbits and their fishing trips and he understood that Jonathan was homesick for the days when they had all been together, sitting around the old table in Sarah's kitchen, as she carefully measured out meagre helpings to each of her children.

No sooner had Jonathan's letter arrived, than Joseph was anxious to relay the news to Solomon in London, whom he knew would be as excited as he was at the prospect of reuniting with Jonathan and Jane again.

Jonathan had requested that Joseph find him a suitable dwelling with some land attached, as he planned to breed ducks. With this in mind, he set off with Jonathan's letter tucked into the top pocket of his jacket, to give Abraham and Ann the good news.

Abraham was well into his eighties and slept most of the day in the old chair close to the fire. Ann was as sprightly as ever and it was she who met Joseph at the door of the house.

"Joseph! Come in! Come in!" she greeted him, opening the door wide which let in a blast of cold air. Abraham stirred in his chair, looking over the top of his glasses to see who had arrived.

Joseph walked over to the chair and grabbed his brother's hand, shaking it warmly as he put his lips close to Abraham's ear.

"I have news, Abe! he said.

Abraham straightened himself up and drew in his legs that were stretched out in front of him.

"What? What was that you said?" Abe asked.

Joseph repeated himself again, watching Abe's face carefully as he spoke.

"I said, I have news for you, Abe."

Abraham nodded, his old, faded eyes staring into Joseph's face as he spoke.

"Oh, yes. What's that, then?" he asked hesitantly.

"A letter came from Australia, Abe, and would you believe, Jon and Jane are coming home."

There was silence in the room. The clock in the hallway struck the hour as Joseph waited for Abraham to digest the news. Ann sprang to her feet and moved quickly over to Abraham's chair. Putting her face close to his, she said, "Did you hear that, Abe? Jon and Jane are coming home from

Australia!" The excitement in her voice carried across the room, as Abraham jerked in his chair.

"Wonderful news, Joe. Ma always wanted him to come home a wealthy man!" he chortled.

Abraham was soon fully awake, as Ann bustled in the kitchen making tea. Joseph spoke again and said, "I'm going over to Longwick next week to look at a property for him. He wants some land to breed ducks."

Joseph laughed at the look that was steadily spreading across Abe's face.

"Breed ducks!" laughed Abraham. "He won't get rich breeding ducks. No money in 'em!"

Joseph put his head back and laughed aloud, as Ann came back into the room carrying a tray of tea and some freshly baked scones.

"This news has put new life into you, Abe," she said gently, lowering her tray onto the table in front of Abraham's chair.

Joseph reached out for a warm scone and said to Abraham, "Our brother's already a wealthy man, Abe. He doesn't need the money."

Both brothers laughed as Abraham continued, "He'll be catching up with Sol, then. He must own half of London by now!"

Abraham was quiet until he spoke again, directly to Joseph, "Next spring you say … he'll be home then? In that case, I want to last until Jon gets here, I'll be happy to see him again."

EPILOGUE

Joseph John sat upright in the old leather chair that had brought comfort to his bone-weary body over the years. He placed his outstretched arms on his desk, caressing the heavily carved oak with his hands, remembering the day he had moved into the office after his father had left for Oxford. Soon afterwards, he had called in the craftsmen and had dark wood panelling fitted to the walls which gave an air of affluence to the room, which he liked.

Helen still occupied the office on the other side of the connecting door, which was filled with her bold designs on heavy vellum sheets and where an aroma of paint, oil, and turpentine mingled to permeate the air with a heaviness that would make it almost impossible for most people to work in such an atmosphere.

Helen was totally unaware, spending long hours of solitude sketching and painting. In latter years, she had taken to portrait painting, her works hanging in the homes and halls of London gentry. She had made quite a name for herself, but in spite of her brother John urging her to seek a more social life, she chose to spend her time alone in her studio.

Louisa had left the workroom when their first child Frank was born, a delicate and sensitive boy. with blond hair and large blue eyes. Frank was soon joined by Eleanor, Rose, and then George, a family which Joseph John looked upon with pride.

As a father, Joseph John wanted the best education London had to offer for his two sons, and at the age of eleven, both boys were enrolled in the prestigious public school that stood in Charterhouse Square, Smithfield, in the centre of London.

Joseph John was a religious man, having given generously of his time to the Wesleyan Chapel that had welcomed him through their doors when he first moved the family into the area. Since those early days, he had worked tirelessly to provide for the needy, setting up soup kitchens and shelters for homeless and destitute people. He preached a life of service to his children, expecting them to follow in his footsteps and to stand beside him in his work.

Joseph John had known Charles Dickens vaguely from the days they both lived in Bloomsbury, and so it was, that when news reached him that Dickens was planning to set up a school in the district for children who were unable to attend the regular schools and who were in need of meals and clothing, he contacted him to offer help from the Wesleyan Chapel, of which he had become an Elder.

The Ragged Schools programme was dedicated to the free education of destitute children and Joseph John immediately saw the need for such a school. He was delighted when Dickens agreed to work with him and soon Joseph's sixteen-year-old daughter, Rose, was teaching at the newly formed school close to their home.

Joseph John was a tireless worker. His artificial flower emporium demanded much of his time, but his dedication to those who truly needed his help left him little time for social occasions. Louisa worked alongside him, as the factory had been passed into the capable hands of a young man who managed with calm efficiency.

For Joseph John and Louisa, it was a hectic but satisfying life. Their four children flourished under Joseph John's strict adherence to the rules he set for them. Both Frank and George performed well at Charterhouse, but all that changed when war with Germany broke out in 1914.

The privileged life Joseph John had built for his family changed overnight when first Frank was called to serve in the army, followed some months later by George. Both men were married by this time, leaving their wives and children behind them as they set off for war.

Wartime in London changed everything and Joseph John threw himself into working for the war effort, trying to keep his mind off of the fear he felt for his two sons fighting in France. Then, in 1916, came the terrible news that George had perished in the Battle of the Somme in France, alongside one million other men.

The agony of grief had taken its toll on the family, in particular Louisa, who struggled constantly to come to terms with the death of her son. Joseph John buried his own grief beneath a mounting schedule of work, but recognised that Louisa required something more to occupy her time, as grief had taken hold of her.

One evening, some months after George's death, Joseph John approached Louisa, with a proposition he had been thinking of for some time. There was a huge demand for a canteen in the area, he explained to his wife, and he would seek permission from the church authorities to use an adjacent building to the Wesleyan Chapel, for such a purpose. This would be a far larger endeavour than anything Louisa had tackled before, when in earlier years she had been involved with a local soup kitchen.

Louisa rose to the occasion and set about finding volunteers to assist in the organisation and running of the canteen. Fresh vegetables were scarce, but it was not long before Louisa had found more volunteers to turn local gardens and flower beds into vegetable patches. Boys in the neighbourhood, who were too young to fight, were allocated gardens to tend.

When the first bomb was dropped on Lincoln's Inn Chapel in Holborn, Joseph John worked tirelessly to set up an army of people to act as air raid wardens. He was at the helm, making himself available to all who needed him. Quickly he became central to the war effort in his part of London, running everything with smooth efficiency.

Louisa began to recover with little time to think about her loss. She was helped by the constant companionship she had found outside her home. A mutual respect and understanding had sprung up between the women who volunteered to help feed those in need; friendships had been carved in the rubble and devastation that had once been a leafy oasis of peaceful calm.

Joseph John and Louisa spent the war years rising to the call of the nation, welcoming home their countrymen who returned shocked and broken, their lungs often attacked with mustard gas from time spent in the trenches. Whenever help was needed, they were both there, determined and organised.

When the war drew to a close in 1918, Joseph and Louisa concentrated on the work to be done to rehabilitate the nation. Their son Frank returned from war, suffering from nightmares that threatened to take away his sanity, and they knew, deep within themselves, that he would never be the same handsome, confident youth who had left for war in 1914.

Joseph John held his head in his hands, thinking sadly of his two sons, one of whom had paid the ultimate price, the other, a shell-shocked young man who would never recover from the horrors of war. Joseph John had mourned the death of his young son many times over and cried for the widow and two young children he had left behind.

When correspondence arrived from His Majesty's Government, in the form of a thick embossed envelope, addressed to himself, in heavy copper-plate handwriting, he had taken the letter opener from his desk and slipped the blade beneath the flap of the envelope.

As the letter sat before him, Joseph John found himself reading the contents over and over again and taking the letter into his hand to look at it once more still. It was to inform him that he was to receive the OBE, for services to his community in the time of war. It gave a date for his investiture at Buckingham Palace. For Louisa, it was a bright moment in a sea of grief and she was looking forward to the coming months.

Joseph John relaxed into the worn leather of his chair, the one place that had given him comfort in the most trying of times, and sent up a silent prayer of thanks for a life that was slowly returning to a more pleasant time, when he would be able to smile again.

Acknowledgements

I am so very grateful to all those who gave their support and encouragement to the writing of this book, especially my family who never lost faith in me. To my editor Beth, whose patience and clear-sightedness helped to create a story worth reading and to Robert New at Tale Publishing, who went out on a limb to become my publisher, which enabled me to tell this story.

Charity number 1122439

www.goodnewschildrenstrust.org.uk

All proceeds from the sale of this book will be donated to Good News Children's Trust (UK).

The Trust works to provide educational opportunities for underprivileged children in Mombasa.

www.ingramcontent.com/pod-product-compliance
Lightning Source LLC
Chambersburg PA
CBHW030256010526
44107CB00053B/1739